One Key: SEE, One Key: DO

accessing your brain's
creative abilities

by Cinse Bonino

ONION
RIVER

PRESS

191 Bank Street
Burlington Vermont 05401

ISBN: 978-1-949066-16-6

Library of Congress Control Number: 2019909875

Publisher's Cataloging-in-Publication Data

Names: Bonino, Cinse, author.
Cooper, Martin, 1928-, foreword author.
Title: One key : SEE , one key : DO : accessing your brain's creative abilities / by Cinse Bonino ; foreword by Martin 'Marty' Cooper.
Description: Burlington, VT: Onion River Press, 2019.
Identifiers: LCCN 2019909875 | ISBN 978-1-949066-16-6
Subjects: LCSH Creative ability. | Creation (Literary, artistic, etc.) | Creative thinking. | Self-actualization (psychology) | Consciousness. | BISAC SELF-HELP / Creativity
Classification: LCC BF408 .B66 2019 | DDC 153.3/5--dc23

Cover art by Mollie Coons, molliecoons.com
Design, layout, and formatting by Kevin Deutermann

Printed in the United States of America
Onion River Press | 191 Bank Street, Burlington, VT 05401

Also by Cinse Bonino:

The Ride of Your Life: *choosing what drives you* (2018)
Relationship Residue (2018)

Deep gratitude to all my former students
who allowed me to crawl around inside their brains

Contents

Foreword

The theme of the Marconi Symposium in Bologna Italy in October 2013 was "The Science of Creative Thinking" and I was seriously distressed. I was assigned to deliver the keynote at the symposium and yet, to me, its theme was an oxymoron. Everyone knows, I thought, that creativity is amorphous and therefore unscientific. I have always believed that whatever creativity I possessed was an obstacle, an impediment to the clear thinking and structure that is so important to us engineers. I understood that it was useful to come up with an original idea from time to time. But I had great difficulty in reconciling the open-mindedness that is essential in the creative process with the certainty associated with the mathematics and procedures that are the basis of engineering.

It did not take long for me to be reeducated. In her energetic and persuasive presentation, Cinse Bonino convinced me that my concept of the creative person was simply wrong, that creativity was not the province of an exclusive few, and most importantly, that the ability to be creative can be learned and enhanced.

I should not have been surprised. After all, Leonardo da Vinci was one of the most creative characters in history and yet he was a superb engineer. But Leonardo was not unique in his ability to be both of these things. Cinse theorized, that day in Italy, that *anyone* can learn to be creative, and then went on to explain that being creative does not exclude the abilities to be methodical and sensible.

This was a great relief to me. I no longer had to go through life assuming that because I enjoyed ideas, because I always wanted to do things differently, that I could also not be a competent engineer. So Cinse opened a new vision to me and, at the same time, corrected an inferiority complex.

Is creativity an important asset in society? Is it even necessary?

People are better off in the world today than at any time in history. We live longer, are healthier, more productive, and more educated than ever. And yet the world is a mess. Too many of our people live in poverty, there is too much intolerance, we can't afford our healthcare, and our educational systems are erratic. We are not going to solve these problems by doing the same things that we have done in the past; new approaches, new ways of thinking are an imperative. And what a shame it would be to exclude segments of our population from participating in these new ways because they are not *creative*.

Behavioral scientists have, for many years, been developing methods to measure the ability of people to learn and to be creative. Here is my interpretation of some of their fascinating conclusions:

- Creativity is not an abstract concept but a concrete and measurable attribute.
- There is no correlation between age and either creative ability, or the ability to learn. Einstein in his 80s was as creative as a curious eight-year-old and had comparable learning ability.
- People who practice creativity and learning retain and expand these abilities; people who do not, lose them.

Cinse Bonino expands these powerful ideas into practice. Hers is not a purely theoretical book, nor is it purely formulaic. Cinse explains that the ability to create is inherent in our brains.

Abstraction is the one thing that our brains do very well and that machines and other animals do very poorly, if at all. She then goes on to define the elements of creativity and provides us with a variety of examples and exercises that mesh with the theoretical understandings. She distinguishes between mere cleverness and genuine impact.

One Key: SEE, One Key: DO – accessing your brain's creative abilities is, in itself, a masterpiece of creativity. It removes the mystery and misinformation about creativity and replaces them with understanding and process. Whether you are learning to be more creative or teaching others, reading this fine book will open doors you never knew existed.

Martin Cooper

Del Mar, California

April 2019

Introduction

Is it possible to improve creative ability?

We've all encountered someone whose ability to think creatively, amazes us. Many of us wish we could unlock our own creative potential and become more like these dazzling, quick witted, so-called out-of-the-box thinkers. But some of us suspect the genetic lottery determines our level of creativity. We worry our creativity capacity is not only predetermined but also set in stone. This could cause us to doubt our ability to increase our creativity.

I believe it is possible to learn to think more creatively. For close to 15 years, I taught college students how to be more creative. These students came from various backgrounds. Many of them were in creative courses of study, but many were not. Some of them walked into my classroom convinced they were already more creative than their classmates and their professor. Others practically drooled in anticipation at the mere possibility of becoming more creative. And there were always a few who had little confidence in a college course's ability to help them increase their level of creativity. These students entered the classroom desperately clutching small sparks of hope.

What's astonishing is that they all became more creative. Did they all become superstars? No. Did they all reach the same level of creative ability? Of course not. They all did learn how to be creative on *purpose*, not just through happy accidents or in mysterious eureka moments. They developed a meta-awareness of what increases creativity for everyone and for them specifically. They learned how to see differently. They learned how to successfully satisfy a specified creative need. They learned to notice what they do that works, and to be able to do it again. They learned to push themselves beyond *clever* to *excellent*. They learned to let go of some amount of judgment and fear. They learned to be willing to be ridiculous if it gets them to radiant. They learned to unlock their creative potential and to carry it forward to multiple areas of their lives.

We all can learn to increase our creativity by developing the skills that comprise the act of thinking creatively. These skills are similar to the ones that help us to make sense of something that is new to us. Practicing and perfecting these skills will help you to think more creatively. Becoming aware of how to use this new skill-set to process information and concepts will enable you to repeat the process whenever you need it. Many people only equate creativity with artistic pursuits or the act of brainstorming, but creative thinking can be an integral part of the analysis, problem solving, and design present throughout much of our daily lives. Or, to put it another way – creative thinking helps us to discover more, to identify the potential of what we have discovered, and to figure out how we can utilize that potential to craft effective solutions in any life situation.

The four steps and the two keys

This book explains how to combine learning principles, creative methods, and intentional awareness to improve your ability to be creative in useful and productive ways. You will become familiar with each of the four steps of the creative process: *notice, explore, connect,* and *choose.* One key to mastering each of these steps is learning new ways to see. The other key is learning what to *do* with what you see. These two keys can unlock your creative potential and let your inner creative genius loose, *if* you're willing to trust the process and yourself.

Unlearning and benefiting from our brain's natural tendencies

Our brains use patterns and sorting to help us to recognize concepts and then link them together to make meaning out of what we encounter. We use prior knowledge and experiences to attach new ideas and concepts to our current understanding in concrete ways. This helps us to make sense of them. We use representations such as metaphors to hold onto the meaning of new abstract concepts. These representations are usually based on things that are already familiar to us. Representations with an emotional component work even better to help new ideas and concepts *stick* with us.

When we create something, we often put pieces of things we're already familiar with together in new ways. In order to do this, we first need to identify and define the need we are trying to satisfy. Then we must locate the things we will use to create our solution, whatever it may be. We start by *noticing* as many things as we can that are available for us to use. Then we *explore* these available things to determine which ones, or which of their parts, seem to have the most potential to help satisfy our current needs. We then *choose* those things and parts of things we believe can be connected in an inventive manner to effectively fulfill our purpose.

All of these steps are important, because if we become overly focused on our end product and hurry through the identification of the conceptual components we need, we won't truly understand what it is we are attempting to create. Without this full conceptual understanding, we might become attracted to things, or parts of these things, that only partially connect to what we need in order to be successful in our creative endeavor. We must learn to refuse to settle for what is falsely enticingly or merely clever; otherwise, we will end up with something flashy but unfinished. But even bad choices sometimes end up being instructive. They can propel us past a solution that only partially fits our needs toward an elegant solution that satisfies our needs in an effective, and perhaps even a unique, manner.

Sometimes we need to pull back the lens to see farther, to allow ourselves to increase our field of sight in order to notice what else is out there. This can only happen if we are willing to take the time to look beyond our initial discoveries. When we do this, we may find something wonderful we didn't initially notice or expect to see. Then it's a matter of sifting through everything we've noticed and determining what seems to have the best possibility of fitting our creative pursuit.

Trusting the process and yourself

Thinking creatively is about searching for what you need for your creative pursuit and being able to recognize it when you find it. If you attempt to *force* an idea or a solution, things tighten up and your creative flow gets reduced to a trickle, or stops completely. Forcing also causes you to lose sight of the concepts you want to satisfy. If you forget what you're trying to do, you may deviate from your actual quest in your rush to get things *done*. If you stop believing in the value of the creative process you might also lose faith in your ability to be creative.

Becoming aware of what works for you

We each need to learn what works best for us – to become intentionally cognizant of our own creative process; to discover what motivates and deters us; to become familiar with our own processing style and communication habits; and to notice our intuitive actions, the ones we want to be able to repeat at will and those we want to will away. Just as a spigot must be open for water to flow freely, we must trust what we've come to learn about our own process and not let stress and pressure tempt us to fall back into old unproductive habits, which can clog our creative flow.

Knowing when you're finished

You can stop your creative process too soon and end up settling for something far less fabulous than you had hoped to achieve. You also can keep going long after you should have stopped and overdevelop something into oblivion. Both are equally undesirable. Learning how to know when you are finished is one of the trickiest aspects of being creative.

Communicating your journey and your creation

You can be wildly and wonderfully creative and never get your work accepted or funded if you are incapable of clearly explaining what you're doing, why you're doing it, and how you're doing it. Someone else's idea might not be as good as yours, but if they do a better job of explaining it, their idea is likely to be the one chosen to advance to development and possible success.

Unlocking your creative potential and releasing your inner genius

A bunch of monkeys playing around with a typewriter might appear to be creative. It has even been humorously suggested that if we gave those monkeys enough time they would eventually type all the works of Shakespeare. Being creative *is* about being playful, but it's also about producing something that will satisfy a given set of conceptual needs. This book can help you to awaken a childlike ability to see in new ways. It can also help you to make useful connections and to learn to sift through choices in a faster, more conceptually focused, and purposeful manner. Finally, this book will attempt to guide you toward becoming more aware of your own process so you can benefit from both conscious and subconscious memories, thoughts, and ideas. If you learn to do this, you may begin to feel as if your creativity is suddenly flowing in a magical way. But it won't be magic making your creativity flow; it will be you. Once you acquire a working set of creative tools, learn to apply them intentionally, and become more cognizant of your own creative process, you will be able to access and ride your creative flow more often and more successfully than you ever have before.

Did you see that?

In order to be creative you need to be able to see more, to notice more. Why? Because what you notice becomes what you will have available to use for your creative pursuit, whatever it might be. It doesn't matter whether you are trying to solve a problem, name a new product, write computer code, concoct a special dessert, or synthesize an advanced chemical compound, you cannot use something if you are not aware it exists. You are also unlikely to end up using something if you aren't currently judging it to be potentially useful for your purposes. These two factors bring us to the deceptively simple First *See* Key Principle:

Choose to see more.

o see more matter? Because until you become
n on any gems, you will need to sift through
to find them. To do this, you need to teach
ch as you can instead of focusing only on
ged to be useful. Train yourself to notice
g regardless of how little you think it has to do with your
project or problem. Don't worry at first if the things you notice
appear to be useful or not. Concentrate on seeing rather than on
judging. Discerning what's good for your purposes will come later.
If you begin to narrow your choices too soon you might miss the
best possible thing. Sure, you may still find something good, but
you could also miss something really great.

If noticing more of what's available increases the odds of finding
something amazing, why do people stop looking and settle for the
first thing that resonates with them? There are a variety of reasons.
Here are a few.

Relief that you found *something*

Sometimes people feel relieved when they find something they
think will work. Secretly, they were quite worried they wouldn't
find something decent or wouldn't find anything usable in time.
What a relief it is when they find something that actually seems
to fit their needs. They finally can relax and stop searching. These
relief-feelers don't bother to question whether there might be something better out there. Why should they? As far as they're concerned they already have what they need.

Real life example:

You have a daughter. She doesn't think she's pretty. In fact, she is
convinced she's ugly and overweight. The truth is she's actually

physically fit and quite lovely. She's also really smart and has been accepted into her first choice college. However, she has a real loser for a boyfriend/girlfriend. This is the only romantic partner she has ever had. They propose and she says *yes.* They want to get married right away. You are devastated and ask her to wait until she has graduated from college. She says she can't. When you ask her why, she says if she waits, her boyfriend/girlfriend might change their mind and not want to marry her. You tell her, if that happens, she should wait for someone who loves and appreciates her more than her current boyfriend/girlfriend does. She responds by asking you, *What if no one else ever wants to marry me?*

Distracted by something that seems to stand out

Some of us get led astray by things that sparkle. It's easy to be enticed by something amusing or unexpected. We can become charmed by a particular aspect of something; we focus in tightly and assume we've found something amazing. We become excited and also blinded to the other possibilities outside of our now narrowed field of vision. We're not choosing what's in our sights because it beat out the other things around it; we're choosing it because it's all we are allowing ourselves to see.

Real life example:

You're downtown after meeting a friend for coffee. On the way back to your car, or as you walk home, you get the urge for an apple. You go into a local food mart. You spot a particularly shiny McIntosh apple in a bin. Which would you be more likely to do:

- pick up the apple, take it to the check-out counter, pay for it, and carry it out of the store with you, or
- pick up the apple and spin it to check if the other side is just as nice as the shiny side that caught your attention?

Lack of confidence in your own abilities

If someone doesn't trust their own judgment they might stop their search and rush to support someone else's discovery or idea. Perhaps they are too quick to believe others' ideas are better than their own, or they might hesitate to put their own idea forward because they don't want to risk the embarrassment of rejection.

Real life example:

You and a companion are finishing up dinner at a restaurant and choosing a movie to go see. You hate horror but really like action and suspense movies. Your companion tells you about a new movie that's an action flick with plenty of suspense. You seem to remember hearing about the movie from a friend. You're pretty sure it's a horror movie. You suggest looking it up on your phone. Your companion assures you that it's definitely not a horror movie and then says if you don't leave right away you'll miss the beginning. You put your phone away and agree to head to the movies.

Impatience

Some people stop looking because they feel they've looked long enough. The excitement of the hunt wears off. It's no longer a juicy pursuit. It's merely another task to complete. They want to be done with this stage of their project *now*.

Real life example:

A mother takes her son shopping for a new winter hat because he recently lost his hat. He often forgets to wear his hat, frequently misplaces it, and then ends up developing an ear infection. They try on hat after hat in the store. He doesn't like any of them. Finally, frustrated, his mother snatches the one he's currently trying on and says, *That's it; we're buying this one.* The boy fusses and complains that the hat is ugly. He says he doesn't want it. Fed up, the mother drags him to the counter and pays for the hat. Guess who won't be wearing their hat very often? Guess who also is probably going to end up with another ear infection?

Finding the perfect thing to satisfy the needs of your creative pursuit can feel daunting. For now, let's not worry about how to determine when it's okay to stop looking, but instead focus on how you can help yourself to *see* more.

In order to see more you must become more observant. This means you need to *notice* more of what you see, to register as much as you can. Think of yourself as a robot scanning an area and cataloging everything it sees. Now imagine the robot has a sense of wonder similar to that of a three-year old child. It is simultaneously capable of analytically listing all it notices and of feeling delighted or curious about each and every thing it sees.

To see *more* is both a skill and a choice. It is something you can learn to do. It is also something you can eventually become adept at doing quickly and naturally; however, initially it is similar to learning to use a muscle in a new way. It can feel awkward or silly. It can even seem pointless. It isn't; you are training yourself to put more creative raw material at your disposal. Here are four ways to become more observant.

Start by noticing what's around you.

This sounds obvious but most of us usually don't do it. It takes conscious effort to investigate your surroundings thoroughly. Think about how that robot would scan an area. Look in front of you. Look to each side. Look behind you. Look up and look down. Do this literally. How often have you walked into a store, or a friend's home, looked up and seen something you had not previously noticed? When you ask how long whatever you've just discovered has been there, you are told it's been there for weeks, for months, or maybe that it's always been there. You didn't notice it because you didn't look up. You didn't look up because you didn't expect to see anything up there. You probably didn't do this consciously, but some thinking part of you decided that looking up wasn't needed in this situation. A robot on the other hand, if instructed to scan the same area would raise and lower or tilt its head to record everything from floor to ceiling. It would cover every square inch as it systematically catalogued the entire location. It would record all 360 degrees of the area. Whether you are looking in a room, a building, a city, a book, a refrigerator, a closet, or a meadow, remember to *make like a robot* and look everywhere.

Look beyond where you are.

Imagine this hypothetical robot also can penetrate walls with x-ray like vision. This would enable it to see people and things beyond the walls that could conceivably come into contact and interact with the people and things the robot has observed in the originally scanned area. Extrapolate and envision anything beyond the borders of your original scan area that could possibly have an impact on something within the area's borders.

Fight the urge to prejudge what you see.

Our brains automatically sort the things we see into categories based on our prior knowledge and experiences. Items with similar characteristics usually end up grouped together. This process can be very helpful when we are being creative. It can also limit our ability to see things in new and different ways. Most of us, when we are looking for something to fulfill a specific need, have a tendency to immediately sort what we see into two categories: *useful* and *not useful*. Often, we unconsciously and immediately reject many of the things we see because our brains have automatically placed them in the *not useful* category. In fact, our brains can slap a *reject* label on so quickly it may not even register that we've gone through this judgment process. We may continue on unthinkingly ignoring multiple items because our brains have deemed them *unsuitable* and therefore unworthy of consideration.

We are also aware of how we intentionally categorize some of the things we notice. Perhaps we purposely decide to reject things we think are boring or ridiculous, or maybe we don't want to choose anything that strikes us as difficult or dangerous. Regardless of which negative attribute we use to dismiss certain possible choices, this behavior ensures that these items have no chance of making it into our *up-for-consideration* pile. To become more observant, we need to intentionally and consciously abstain from this presorting process. Put your judgment on hold. Stay open, scan, and notice all that is available for you to consider using.

Look inside your own mind.

Do the robot style scanning internally too. This is where that three-year old sense of wonder comes into play. Consider your past experiences, early memories, books, movies, stories others have told you, emotional responses, anything you recall or think of as you view what you see around you. Make a mental or physical note of these things too.

But, before you attempt to use any of these methods to *see more*, give yourself permission to look ridiculous. This is the First *Do* Key Principle:

Be willing to appear ridiculous.

This is difficult for many of us. We worry about losing our credibility. We are concerned people might judge us poorly or fail to take us seriously if we put forward an idea they regard as silly or not worth considering. We also care deeply about how we see ourselves. We don't want our inner self to feel ashamed or to harbor regrets. These are all legitimate concerns. Being authentic can be risky. How do we find the courage to suggest ideas or solutions we fear others may initially misjudge or ultimately ridicule? We need to care more about bringing an idea we believe could turn out to be uniquely excellent to everyone's attention than we care about avoiding any potential ridicule or judgment that could come our way. If we overfeed our fear of being judged, it may cripple our creativity by convincing us to avoid anything that seems risky, no matter how inventive or excellent it may be. If you don't take risks you'll never unlock your true potential – not during your work on a specific creative project, and not in your overall creative practice. You *can* improve your creativity without being willing to appear ridiculous, but you'll probably never be the incredibly creative person you aspire to be. You have to be open to let more in. When you're open you're vulnerable. Think of it as the physics of creativity:

- Being open makes you vulnerable.
- Being vulnerable increases your ability to *see*.
- Increasing your ability to see multiplies your options.
- Multiplying your options enables you to be more selective.

- Being more selective allows you to notice ways to make new connections.
- New connections can be used to create something new.

Creating something new involves putting things – thoughts, ingredients, components, or whatever – together in a new way. The design or plan for how you will ultimately decide to put things together will be based on the new meaning you create using the new connections you discovered. And this new meaning must satisfy your creative pursuit's needs and fulfill each objective in a readily recognizable way. If you want to create something dazzling and unforgettable, your audience has to *get* it, to understand it. It has to make sense to them in a relatable way. They have to recognize and comprehend what you have created, or it will fall flat.

Being willing to look ridiculous can improve your ability to *see* exponentially, because you can see more when you stop worrying about failing or looking stupid.

EXERCISES
to help you see more

Exercise 1:
Keep a creative See More journal

Use the topics listed at the end of these instructions, or your own topics, to make daily entries in a journal or blog. Consider the same topic for an entire week. Try to write something about the topic each day.

On the first day, open your journal and write whatever initially comes to mind when you consider the week's topic (the topic: *Looking Down* for example). Concentrate on noticing more. First do this internally. Notice the thoughts and memories that come to mind when you think about the topic. Maybe you'll remember something someone said at a party or a scene from a movie you saw recently or years ago. Perhaps something from your child-hood or a dream you once had will resurface. Whatever it is, write it down. Think about the topic within the contexts of both nature and the man-made world – in your home, at work, or when you are walking or driving. Notice what you see, hear or overhear, say, taste, and feel. Don't judge what comes to mind, just write it down. You cannot get this wrong. And don't worry about spelling or grammar; you can always edit your writing later if you want to use it for something. For now, just concentrate on recording your thoughts.

On the second day, go back to the first day's entry and write whatever the contents of the entry make you think of. Remember, don't judge. Simply record whatever pops into your mind when you read what you wrote down the previous day. Perhaps something you wrote about looking down into the Grand Canyon makes you think of the burros some people ride down the trails into the canyon. Notice whether you hesitate to record your initial thoughts because of wanting to come up with something better. Try to stick with and record the first thoughts you have. Then write a new response about the week's original topic. This is your entry about the topic for the second day.

On the third day, you will respond to the second day's entry by writing whatever it makes you think of, and you will also write a new response to the week's original topic. If you have the time and inclination to do this every day, that's great, if not, try to do it at least two or three times during the week. This will help you to think about the topic in multiple ways. It will help you to more thoroughly *robot search* your environment, experiences, and memories for ideas and concepts that connect to the week's topic.

Below are examples of journal entries from three days and potential topic ideas to get you started.

Creative journal example for Day 1 Looking Down entry:

Day 1 entry – *Looking down* makes me think of how I look down at steps when I am going up or down a stairway. I do this because the lenses in my glasses are for both near and far vision correction. The bottom part helps me to see close and the top part to see further away. I need to look through the bottom to see the steps well enough to maintain my balance. People often think I'm looking down because I'm shy or because I'm stuck up and think I'm better than they are.

Creative journal example for response to Day 1 and for Day 2 Looking Down entry:

Response to Day 1 – Yesterday's entry about my glasses makes me think about how we sometimes think people are judging us, or looking down on us, when actually they aren't. Maybe they look at us with a funny expression on their face that we read as disdain but actually they're trying to remember where they met us before because we look familiar to them. Or maybe they ate something that disagreed with them or they are on their way to a meeting they'd rather avoid. This also makes me think of how people often say nice things about someone to other people but don't tell the person themselves the nice thing. Why do people do that?

Day 2 entry – I don't mind looking down from high places. It doesn't scare me at all. I like looking over cliffs and from a seat at the top of a Ferris wheel. But I do not like looking through cracks and seeing something far, far, below me. It doesn't make any sense but it makes me feel as if I could get sucked down through the crack and then fall down into that great distance below me. I even get scared when I walk between trains or drive over bridges that have a grated road surface.

Creative journal example for response to Day 2 and for Day 3 Looking Down entry:

Response to Day 2 – My entry about cracks made me think about how cracks are often more interesting than the things on either side of them. Cracks separate. Cracks provide a way in. Cracks can show vulnerability or the wisdom of age. Cracks can cause accidents. Cracks can help you open something to get to something special inside. Safecrackers destroy the safe to get to the money or jewels inside. Nutcrackers destroy the nut's shell to get to its meat. And someone's coldness or bitterness can crack and allow them to connect with another human being, can enable them to let love in.

Day 3 entry – People sometimes look down instead of looking you in the eye because they are lying to you. But other times, people look down because what they're saying is so true that it frightens them to think that you won't believe them. Still other times people look down because you have more power than they do in the situation. Body language can tell us so much and yet we can misinterpret it completely because people not only speak different languages, their bodies do too.

Some topic suggestions to jumpstart your own selections:

looking down, footsteps, cake, things that annoy you, permission, juice, shiny things, habits and other automatic behaviors, eyebrows, childish things, laziness, indecency, clowns, things which bring comfort, rhythm, unexpected occurrences, dirt, practice, freedom, perfection, fear, different types of connections, the color red, peculiar things, air, innocence, anger, farm animals, fair play, secrets, masks, appetites, disappointments, purity, truth, pointy things, magic, lies people tell themselves, itchiness, cold, water, perceptions of power, hope, ogres, sounds and noises, kindness, running away, speed, bad smells, curiosity, kind words, lost and found, caution, comfort food, commitment, conformity, embarrassment, wishes, intelligence, escalation, buried treasure, justice, joy

Exercise 2 Version 1:
Scan and note your surroundings

Go into a room in your home and choose a category; make up your own or use one of the suggested sample category labels below. Scan the room and notice everything that could conceivably fit into that particular category. Make a written or mental list of each thing you see.

Repeat the process, only this time stand on a stepstool or chair. Slow yourself down. Notice how you choose to scan the room. Do you go back-and-forth or up-and-down in a particular direction, or do you turn in a circle as you scan? Add any additional items you notice to your original list.

Repeat the process again, this time from a seated or lying position directly on the floor. Scan the room differently than you did last time. If your eyes previously went back-and-forth, this time make them go up-and-down or around in a circle. Then scan again using your original method. Notice what happens. Once again, add any new items you notice to your list.

Some category label suggestions to help you generate your own:

> things made of metal, things made of wood, things made of plastic, round things, things with corners, edible things, things that can spill, dangerous things, gifts, soft things, things someone might steal, quiet things, things that burn easily, things with many parts, things you can share, controversial things, things often borrowed, mechanical things, sharp things, sophisticated things, scary things, heavy things, traditional things, frivolous things, unexpected things, things you might mail, things in a series or a set, unique things, musical things, snooty things, things that cover other things, stuffed

things, old things, things which could make you cry, smelly things, things with patterns, things you put other things inside of, tools, things that move, things that can melt, things that fasten, things you twist

Exercise 2 Version 2:
Scan and note your surroundings

Go to a public place either indoors or out. Start by observing the people you see around you. Notice how many instances of a predetermined attribute you can spot among the people you observe. It doesn't matter what attribute you pick – it can be people with curly hair, bags worn cross-body, or shoes with colored laces, or whatever – simply sit or stand in a given area and make a mental note each time you notice another instance of the characteristic you have chosen. You can do this exercise while you are walking too. Once again, take note of *how* you scan. Are you looking randomly? Is there a pattern to your surveillance? What seems to work best for you?

Do the exercise again, only this time, explore the inanimate objects around you not associated with people. Notice particular colors or patterns around you on signs, walls, doors, sidewalks or flooring, or on any other object around you. Grocery stores provide an object-rich environment for doing this.

Finally, put on earphones and listen to music, or put in earplugs and attempt to notice the different types of nonverbal communication happening around you. Label the first one you see. Is it anger? Disapproval? Happiness? Love? Impatience? Whatever you see, note it and then look for additional instances of this same nonverbal message. Uncover your ears and continue to look. Do you find the exercise easier with or without sound?

Choose a second form of nonverbal communication to notice and repeat the recording process. Then cover your ears again and repeat the exercise. Finally, notice how time is represented around you. Notice speed, slowness, lack of concern about time, a frantic rushing, and anything else that appears to be a physical representation of time. See how many different representations of time, both actions and objects, you can notice.

Exercise 3:
Generate an attributes list

Pick an object to consider. It could be something from your pocket or from a drawer in your kitchen. It could be a statue or shrub in a park. It doesn't matter. Decide on any object – just make sure you can view it easily. Use a notebook or a computer and list five things you notice about the object. Start with the object's most obvious physical characteristics.

Keep looking at the object and list five more things you notice about it. Keep doing this until you have listed 50 things about the object.

As you write your list you can shift to describing the object in comparison to other objects in an *it's-bigger-than-a-breadbox* manner. Once you have exhausted listing the object's physical characteristics, you can move on to listing how the object could be used. A statue could provide a place to hang your hat or coat. It doesn't matter whether anyone *would* actually use the object in the ways you generate, just that they *could* use it that way.

If you still haven't reached 50 characteristics, note what the object reminds you of. A shrub might remind you of a particular type of hairstyle for example.

Exercise 4:
Notice what you usually miss

Pick something random to notice. You could choose to intentionally pay attention to all the doorknobs and handles you encounter today or perhaps notice all the buttons on people's clothing. Take the time to notice something you don't usually focus your attention on. Check out everyone's eyebrows. Notice their ears. Are they big? Small? Flabby? Wrinkled? Do they have big lobes or hardly any lobes at all? Notice if the people around you, not just the ones you know, are right-handed or left-handed. Notice all the slip-on shoes. Notice the height difference in the couples and small groups of people you encounter. Notice the things people do when other people are speaking.

Notice random things about you and your immediate surroundings. Pay attention to how you place your foot on the ground when you take a step forward. Notice where you put your weight when you are standing still. Notice the direction your eyes glance when you are trying to remember something. Notice what you do with your hands when you walk. Notice the sounds you hear. Notice the background sounds we often miss such as very quiet heating or venting noises. Also notice what you hear from your own body – both internal noises and the sounds your body and clothing make as you move through space.

Most of all, notice what you *think and do* as you attempt to see more. What works for you? What makes you feel really awkward and renders you less effective? Do you do or say anything that makes these exercises more difficult to do? What makes you feel a bit foolish but really seems to work well? Figure out what you do intuitively that helps you to notice more. Make a note so you can do it on purpose in the future.

Notes:

2

Leap before you look.

Most of our lives we have been told to *stay on track*, to pay attention. We probably got in trouble if we daydreamed in school. We may have noticed that most people have a tendency to get irritated if we suddenly change the subject during a conversation. We're told: *Focus. Get serious. Do what you're told.* We have learned linear thinking is usually favored in educational and professional settings. We also may have noticed that it is often expected in many social situations as well. In the workplace, a person who thinks aloud in a non-linear fashion is more likely to be seen as a slacker or as stupid because others may perceive them to be going *off task*; whereas socially, someone who goes off topic is often perceived to be rude or disrespectful. This can be a problem when you want, need, or are required to be creative. Staying on track by following customary, expected patterns of thinking usually takes you to the usual, expected destinations. Tracks are fixed. The train doesn't take a detour through the countryside; it stays on the rails and shows up at the station, and people expect it to get there at the pre-determined time. They value the safety of predictability over the uncertainty of new experiences.

Often, when we are asked to be creative, especially at work, we delight in being able to take fabulous detours of thought away from the expected. This is what they asked us to do, right? Apparently not, because suddenly everyone, or almost everyone, or at least the head decision maker, tells us to get back on track. They don't want us taking any detours. This is confusing. They don't seem willing to go on a journey with us toward a deliciously different and excellent idea. What's more, they may expect us to quickly arrive at a fully developed product or solution. They don't understand the path to excellence is rarely a straight shot. They want us to *be* creative without allowing us to *think* creatively.

Understand why other people get nervous when we come up with innovative ideas.

People may get nervous if we begin to deviate from what they expect us to do, even if we've already proven ourselves to be highly skilled at being enormously creative in the past. They worry because they aren't able to see our destination. They are concerned because we often don't appear to have a map or a plan. Instead we seem to be following a set of clues they can't see. They don't trust our process because they think it looks like an arbitrary series of magical bursts of inspiration. It's not. Not exactly. What's actually happening is a good thing – a whole lot of synaptic leaps and bursts of connections are forming in our brains. Some we are aware of and others we are not. Trusting these bursts helps us to be creative. To be truly innovative you have to learn to trust them with no map, no track, and no seatbelt. Doing this is like freefalling and teleporting toward a quick whiff of a scent from a good trail. You have to follow the scent to get where you need to go. You know *conceptually* where that is but you don't have exact directions. If your directions are too precise you'll become convinced you need to stay on the main path and then you may never notice what you most want to find. Instead, choose to learn how to leap, how to follow what you sense to be inexplicably *right* or helpful, even if you don't know why you think this is so. In other words, you need to follow the Second *Do* Key principle:

Don't stay on track.

Get off track in a good way.

The secret to not staying on track is to go wherever your brain leads you instead of in the direction that habit, media influences, or other preprogrammed expectations compel you to choose. In order to listen to your own mind you have to ignore the insistent inner voice that tries to push you toward what is expected. This takes intentional effort because most of us have a prewired response to believe our overly-acculturated inner voice, and once we believe it, we usually do what it tells us to do. It's hard to silence the voice. You can't simply turn it off. It's in your head demanding to be heard. And it's very good at delivering a convincing spiel. First it gives you *the* answer. It's the logical, natural answer. Of course it is. It's what almost everyone will come up with because it's *so* obvious. It isn't horrible; it just isn't very good. It probably fits what you are looking for in one glaringly apparent way, but it probably doesn't satisfy what your project needs in various other ways. The voice will not point this out. The voice will tell you this proffered idea is perfect. Then it will warn you that if you don't pick the idea it suggests, you won't be able to come up with anything better. It will try to scare you, whispering: *You don't want to fail, do you?* It will try to sound as if it is looking out for you: *If you don't hurry up and tell this idea to everyone, someone else will and then they'll get the credit instead of you.* The voice is very persuasive. It knows how to tailor its arguments so all your buttons are pushed, and it knows just how much pressure to apply. It's also persistent. It delivers its message on a replay loop that never ends. This voice is not your friend. But the voice is right about something. You do need to pay attention to what the voice is telling you. It isn't the right answer, but it *is* the first step on the way to a very good answer.

Start with what is obvious.

There's nothing wrong with initially thinking of what is most obvious. You're not trying to start with something unique and amazing; you're trying to find it. We usually need to get past all the things we think of automatically in order to get to the things that are different and more interesting than the same-old-same-old. One of the major influences we need to get past is the media. It is amazing how many sounds and images bombard us every day. These media creations are designed to convince us to do or not to do something, or to believe or to stop believing something. They are also designed to be very *sticky*. Most of us can effortlessly hum tunes from commercials and finish slogans. When asked what word first comes to mine when I say *headache*, for many people it's the name of a particular pain reliever. Why? Because advertisements are repeated so many times we become prewired to leap to them. These auto pathways are similar to the muscle memories we often experience in our daily lives. My tennis forehand became consistently effective once I repeated good strokes often enough to create dependable muscle memory. Similarly, after working at the same place for several years, I could correctly key in my long distance code on the phone without recalling the numbers on the keys I was pressing.

There are other kinds of habitual responses. If I say *cold*, you probably think *hot*. *Cat* elicits *dog* and so on. Opposites are another type of response many of us think of first. Don't dismiss these auto-responses; they make good launching pads for better leaps. Rhyming words are another auto-response. I'm not sure if it's because of all those picture books we read as children – think *Dr. Seuss* – but most of us also leap fairly quickly to words that rhyme.

Use obvious auto-responses as springboards for developing inventive ideas.

Trying to stop these auto-responses can be difficult. What's easier and more helpful is to let them wash through, and then out of, your mind. Don't fight them. Acknowledge them. Be entertained by them. Notice if you react strongly – positively or negatively – to any of them. Over time you'll get through them much more quickly. You'll also learn to zero in on any good concepts hiding inside of these unremarkable initial responses.

It doesn't matter what you're trying to create. It could be a product name, something to make for dinner, or a new way to build something. You can always use your first obvious ideas to help you leap toward something better. Let's say you were trying to think of a name for a new sleep medication. (Although we're using a product as an example here, this process applies to any naming endeavor.) All the usual auto-responses will arise. What comes to mind when you think of sleep? Those of us who are visual might think of the string of *Zs* that usually appears over a sleeping cartoon character's head. Expressions people use all the time also tend to pop up: *catch some Zs, sleep like a log* or a *stone*, and *sleep tight*. We may also remember traditional childhood bedtime sayings: *nightly night, sweet dreams, time to go nuh-nuh*, and *don't let the bedbugs bite*. Other terms used for sleep might also occur to you: *shut eye, downtime*, or *sawing logs*. Then of course there are slightly more extreme expressions of a good night's sleep: *sleep like the dead, down for the count,* and *out like a light.* Most of these probably would be a little too out there to be used as the name of a sleeping aid; however, they would be familiar to people who are in the market for a good night's sleep. While it's helpful for the name to contain familiar elements, it also has to grab a buyer's attention. It needs to have enough juiciness to be interesting while simultaneously representing the concept being sold in a discernible and recognizable way. This sense of familiarity is important because it will help the name stick with buyers. But first, we need to identify the concepts we want to consider for this product.

Sift through your initial ideas to find useful concepts.

Let's see if we can find some familiar concepts in those auto phrases that popped up. *Down time, shut eye, catch some Zs, saw some logs,* and *go nuh nuh* all represent crossing over to a different state of being. While *sleeping like a log* or a *stone, sleep tight, out like a light, down for the count,* and *sleep like the dead* all imply being in a deep state of sleep. *Don't let the bedbugs bite* and *sweet dreams* indicate a pleasant experience. We also know the buyer wants to fall asleep easily with no ill side- or aftereffects. These concepts along with something familiar the buyer can recognize will result in a good name. The makers of NyQuil® have a sleep aid they call ZzzQuil®. This is a fabulous name. The NyQuil® brand is already associated with ease of use, no side effects, and slipping comfortably into sleep. The *Zzz* at the front of the name communicates in an immediately recognizable manner that this elixir will get you those elusive Zs. NyQuil® advertises itself as a *nighttime cold and flu medicine that helps you sleep*; we're told DayQuil® is the same good stuff without the drowsy factor so we can take it during the day; and now ZzzQuil® will make us float pleasantly to sleep with no unnecessary medications or habit forming side effects. If they had chosen to call it *ZQuil*, with just one *Z*, it would not have carried the same meaning as with *Zzz*. Those multiple Zs are immediately recognizable as sleep. Vicks® nailed it. Of course they already had product recognition going for them, but you can see how they addressed all the important concepts.

Apply conceptual thinking in order to repurpose and create something new.

But what if instead of needing to create something out of words and letters we needed to create something out of actual physical *things* around us? Here's a real life example. Many years ago I lived out in the country near a lake. It was midday on July fourth and we were getting the yard ready for a party. Our guests, about 25 of them, were coming later that afternoon. Once they all arrived, we would sit down together for dinner outside, and then watch the fireworks scheduled to go off across the lake when it became dark enough. Later, when the bugs became overly zealous, we'd head indoors. We'd make music with the various instruments several people had brought, and sing until the younger children started to fall asleep. My parents, who were visiting from out of state, were helping my son and I get ready for the party. We placed tables end-to-end to so we could eat banquet style. We arranged chairs around the tables and left spaces for the additional chairs some of the guests would bring. The oil torches were refilled and someone good at making fires laid kindling and logs in the outdoor fireplace.

I got help carrying a huge stainless steel urn, about 32 inches tall and a foot in diameter, outside. The urn was beautifully made and obviously of commercial quality. I had picked it up at a garage sale for $5.00. I was proud of finding it and of paying so little for it. The best thing about it was the spigot at the bottom you could flip open to fill your glass. We put it on the drinks table with the spigot hanging out over the edge above the grass. We dumped in pitchers of lemonade and ice until it was full. A little while later my dad called me over to the urn. He pointed at the spigot that now had a steady drip. The drip rate was such that we were losing lemonade fairly quickly. My dad asked me if I had a rubber washer. I told him no. My dad asked if I had a junk drawer. This was a loaded question. My dad believed in having a drawer or a box into which you should throw anything you didn't currently have a use for but that might come in handy one day in the future, even if you couldn't identify or name the doohickey you had decided to keep. I told my dad that of course I had a junk drawer and we went to check it out. My dad scanned all the items in the drawer but found nothing of use. He paused and thought for a moment. Then he asked me if I had an old rubber glove. I told him yes. He took the glove I handed to him and snipped off the end of one of its fingers. He then cut a second piece from that same finger. This cut created a rubber ring. He took apart the spigot, squished in the newly created rubber *washer* until it fit well, reattached the spigot, and no more drip.

Analyze the leaping path.

So what made my dad, a mechanical engineer, think of using an old rubber glove to create something to solve our problem? Here's what I think happened. First he thought of a rubber washer because that's what is *usually* used in the case of a leaky spigot. If there had been a hardware store handy that was open on the Fourth of July, we could have zipped out and purchased one of the correct size. But there wasn't.

Next he leapt to wondering what could be used instead of a rubber washer. His mechanical engineer's mind first focused on the *concept* of shape. Then he began to think of where his daughter might keep something that resembled the ring shape of a rubber washer. This brought him to the junk drawer, the most likely place to find an odd little doohickey resembling a rubber washer in his daughter's home. This also turned out to be a dead end.

Then my dad relaxed and let his mind free associate. He let himself *see* more. He thought about the washer and the fact that it was rubber. Thinking about rubber made him leap to rubber gloves. Why? They probably popped into his mind since they were also made of rubber and were something his daughter was also likely to have around. (My dad keyed in on the concept of *material* rather than *shape* here.) But then, instead of dismissing the rubber gloves for being *unfit*, he kept thinking about them. Then his brain made the final creative leap. He realized that even though the gloves were nothing like a washer, they were made of rubber and he might be able to create a washer from them. This led him to the idea of cutting the tip off of one of the fingers on the glove and then cutting a *ring* from the top portion of that same finger.

All of this happened rather quickly once he thought of the rubber gloves. The only reason he was able to come up with this idea was because he didn't dismiss the rubber gloves when he first thought of them. Instead, he considered them for a few nanoseconds more, just long enough to discover where his leap had taken him. In other words, first he leapt to the rubber gloves and then he looked at where he had landed to see if it was of any value. And again, it's important that he stayed at that landing place long enough to truly assess its worth. In this case it was mere seconds. It might have taken him longer if he wasn't a mechanical engineer who was already predisposed to think about materials and shapes and their functions.

I knew my dad well enough that when he asked if I had any rubber gloves, I immediately realized he had come up with a solution. It took me a few more seconds to figure out his plan. My dad would not have been discouraged had I disparaged his request for a rubber glove. He was looking for a solution, not for approval. He didn't care if his idea sounded stupid or ridiculous. This also helped him to think more clearly and broadly.

My father's first hurdle was to stop thinking about things shaped like a ring. If he simply auto-sorted the things around him into *rings* and *not rings*, he never would have thought of the glove. He had to stop himself from limiting his search to only ring-shaped objects.

Then he had to start thinking conceptually. What are the concepts, the attributes of a rubber ring? It fits around the inside of the spigot and it works because it's made of rubber. From those concepts he needed to let himself leap to anything in the surrounding area that mirrored any attribute he had decided to focus on, in this case rubber. He could have decided rubber gloves were too ridiculous and leapt right past them. Or, he might have simply judged the idea to be unworkable. Fortunately for my lemonade he did neither of these things. Sometimes when an idea makes you groan with disdain it can actually mean something good is hiding there. Remember to look where you land when you leap.

Learn to follow your thought urges to leap more successfully.

Tap into whatever associations come up for you when you think conceptually. Some of your thoughts will seem random. Others will obviously be from memories or experiences you've had. Still others will creep toward your inner vision as if they are hiding on the periphery of your consciousness. You'll see or think of only part of something. You'll need to turn your attention more fully toward these things in order to see what your mind is suggesting. It will be like a memory you can't quite grasp, a name you can almost remember, or a fleeting image from a dream. Stop, change direction and follow the trail of whatever is trying to get your attention.

You're thinking of it for a reason. It most likely *fits* a concept you are exploring even if you don't yet recognize how. Be sure to pause and check out anything that feels as if it has juice, or feels zesty and interesting. You might not understand why it feels like a good thing; others might even tell you it isn't, but if it's calling to you, stop and examine it. It might be good or it may lead you to the next idea that moves you forward on your journey toward your final idea or solution.

Be aware of your leaping path.

It's important to know how you got to your ultimate idea for two reasons. First, when things work out well, you want to understand what you did that worked so you can do it again, on purpose, next time. Likewise, if things don't work out so well, you want to try to get a clue about what to do differently in the future. Notice how you allowed yourself to leap. Notice if you stayed stuck for any length of time because you wouldn't let yourself go beyond typical auto-responses. Notice where you prejudged your ideas and where you didn't. Notice what helped you to be willing to leap without looking. Congratulate yourself if you were willing to jump creatively without a parachute of practicality. Learn from observing your own process. When I described my dad's process for arriving at fashioning a rubber washer from a rubber glove, I was showing you what worked for him. It may have been somewhat instructive in helping you to do something similar; however, if it had been your own journey and you were recounting it, it would have been even more useful to you.

Explaining how you arrived at your final idea can also convince someone your idea is a good one. It may be your manager or boss, your customer or client, your producer or director, or even yourself. People are comforted by understanding *how* you arrived at your idea. Even if they are in favor of the idea, it makes them feel better when they understand how you got there. If they are on the fence about your idea, hearing about your journey just might push them over to your side of things.

Learn to leap with others.

This process of leaping and then looking where you've landed gets even more interesting when you do it with others. Most people call this brainstorming. Brainstorming can be very productive. It can also be a lot of talk that generates very little of any actual use after expending an enormous amount of energy and effort. You need all the key ingredients mentioned above (and listed below) for a good brainstorming session whether you're working with others or on your own. Of course, when you do it with others it can vastly improve leaping potential because you will have many more memories and associations to leap to and from than when there is only one brain involved. In order to brainstorm successfully everyone needs to agree to:

- Acknowledge auto-responses and use them to leap to other ideas instead of instantly rejecting them or getting stuck on them.
- Think about the aspects of what your project or task requires in a conceptual way.
- Leap to wherever these concepts take you, without prejudging where you land.
- Stay at your leap landing sites long enough to assess what you see there in order to determine if they might be useful in any way.
- Don't turn away from something because you've immediately labeled it as ridiculous or impractical.
- Pay special attention to anything that gives you a strong reaction – either positive or negative – and check those things out just a little while longer.

Of course, you also need to respect the other people you brainstorm with. When someone is on a leaping flow, go along with them for the ride. Notice where they're headed and help them move forward if you can, instead of trying to change their path. Expect others to do the same for you. Most importantly, refrain from labeling someone else's leaps as ridiculous or impractical until you understand *why* they've leapt there, even if they themselves don't initially know why. Get good at showing each other your paths while you're on them. The more people who understand what's happening in any given moment, the more minds can add to the flurry of energy carrying the leaps along. Also be mindful of allowing each other enough time to assess where the leaps have taken you. Park and save any good ideas; they might become new leap-off points if other leaps don't pan out. Stay conceptual in your thinking. Don't panic if you don't find something right away. Brainstorming is about coming up with lots of thoughts to carry you closer and closer to a good idea. Focus on the process. If the process is allowed to work, you will find what you need. If you try to force an idea to emerge, you will likely hit a lot of dead ends. A good end comes from an energy-infused, free flowing process. A bad end, or sometimes a dead end, is often the result of trying to beat a lifeless idea into some semblance of a finished product or solution.

EXERCISES
to help you leap

Exercise 1:
Create a brain train leaping list

Most of us are familiar with the phrase, *train of thought* – we usually think of it as when one word makes us think of the next logical word, and then the next logical word generated from that word, and so on for the entire string of words. Some people call this *word association*. This exercise consists of creating a train of thought that is not based on a logical progression for the entire string of words but rather on the leaps you make from one word to the next because of *your* life experiences. Creating a *brain train* will also help you to get past many auto-responses such as media influences, and go-to responses such as opposites and rhyming. Don't try to force a particular outcome; simply follow the directions and notice what happens.

Exercise 1 Version 1:
Brain train part 1

Number the left side of a piece of paper from 1 to 50 with one number on each line. You can also use a computer screen. Pick a random word to be your first word. Point to a word you see in a book or a magazine, select a word you hear in a song you're listening to, or choose a word in any random way you'd like. Write this word on the first line. Then, immediately write the next word that comes to your mind on the second line. On the third line write the word that the *second* word makes you think of. Try not to think about the first word, just about the second word while writing the third word. Don't worry if you do think about both the first and the second word in order to get to the third word. You might combine the meaning of the first two words based on a particular memory. Don't judge what happens; simply continue to write the words down as they come. Don't skip any words that pop up in your mind. Don't worry if they seem inappropriate or too prescribed. Just keep writing the next word you think of down, one after the other. Go as fast as you can. Try not to repeat any words. Try not to use phrases, just single words. Think as little about the exercise as possible while you are doing it. Just get it done.

Writing such a long list will help you to get beyond auto-responses to other less expected ideas. Keep this in mind when you are brainstorming. Just as you supposedly have to kiss a lot of frogs to find your prince or princess, you need to think of a lot of duds before you find a gem of an idea. Once you learn to do this, you can become more proficient at doing it more quickly. You'll learn to ignore dead end ideas and to zero in on juicy ideas that help you to leap to truly excellent ideas.

Exercise 1 Version 1:
Brain train part 2

As soon as you are done writing the fiftieth word, pick a string of five consecutive words from your list. Numbers 33, 34, 35, 36 and 37 for example. Try to capture what you were thinking about as you leapt from number 33 to number 34, then from 34 to 35, 35 to 36, and 36 to 37. Notice if you thought of a word that you didn't write. Perhaps you wrote *dog* for number 33 and *cat* instantly came to mind as its opposite for word number 34. Then you thought about how your friend Paul is allergic to cats so you wrote *allergies* for word number 35. Notice that you chose to write *allergies* instead of *Paul* or *friend*. There would be nothing wrong with doing this; it's just interesting and helpful to notice what you did. Why? Because you didn't capture *friend* or *Paul* initially, but you became aware of them once you retraced your steps. This is another way that noticing your creative journey can help you. It can keep useful ideas from falling through the cracks. One of those hidden ideas might be the springboard that leads you to a truly excellent, final idea.

Exercise 1 Version 2:
Brain train with friends

If you have three to seven willing friends, do the brain train exercise aloud together before you do it on paper. Stand in a circle. The first person says a random word. The person to their left says the first word that occurs to them. Then the third person says a word based solely on the second person's word and so on the whole way around the circle. Go around the circle two or three times. Make sure everyone knows what to do before you start. Try not to edit yourselves. Say whatever comes to mind. Take turns going first. Notice what happens. Do people seem to say words based only on the word said just before their turn, or do they respond to a word said previously? Do any of you get nervous and worry about what to say? What kinds of auto-responses occur?

Exercise 2:
Make up a story based on five random objects

Choose five random objects and place them on a table or desk. Use them to write a simple, very short story based on the attributes of the objects and what associations those attributes cause you to leap to. The goal isn't to write a really good story but rather to use the attributes of the objects as starting points to leap to ideas you might not have thought of without them.

After you've chosen your objects, think about what each could represent in the story. Think of the characteristics you notice about each object and what concepts you can leap to from them. Here is an example:

Five objects

- a cell phone
- a keychain with a VW symbol on it
- a book of matches from a bar called *Mike's Place*
- a paper clip
- a small pocket knife

The cell phone might make you think of:

Calling someone:
phoning someone, yelling to get someone's attention, connecting to someone, writing to someone, receiving a message from someone, sending someone a psychic message

Hearing a sound:
a buzzing sound, an insect, a warning sound, a secret signal

Music:
a concert, a song, lyrics from a song, having rhythm, whistling or playing music

Electronic signals:
pulses, conspiracy theories, big brother, towers, space, aliens

IDs:
identity theft, secure or secret information, access codes, passwords

People:
friends, family, colleagues, strangers, telemarketers

The keychain with a VW symbol on it might make you think of:

Transportation:
cars, road trips, travel, commuting, traffic, traffic accidents, speeding tickets

Germany:
lederhosen, beer, steins, Europe, imported goods, tariffs and taxes, smuggling, shipping

Names with the initials VW:
such as *Victor Winters, Valerie Welch*

Company names:
such as *Volkswagen, Villain Ware, Vacation World*

Keys:
unlocking, locks, secrets, quests, treasure hunts

Discs:
magic buttons, badges of honor, travel tokens

The book of matches from a bar called Mike's Place might make you think of:

Drinking:
beer, mixed drinks, wine, drunkenness, brawls, broken bottles, fun times with friends, peanuts, pretzels, chips, bartenders

Fire:
light, pyromaniacs, candles, burnt smells, getting burned, forest fires, fire fighters, fire trucks, fighting fire with fire

Smoking:
tobacco, smoking controlled substances, pipes, roll your own, prisons, taxes, cartons, duty free

Igniting:
the flame of desire, burning the candle at both ends

Books:
libraries, homework

Covers:
closing and opening, hidden, jackets

Advertising:
billboards, messages, skywriting

Memos:
phone numbers, directions, important notes

Names:
people you know named *Mike*

Entertainment:
microphones and other AV equipment

The paper clip might make you think of:

Connections:
attachments, closeness, groupings

Twisting:
bending, meandering, wandering, walking in circles, mazes

Metal:
shininess, sparkling, reflections

Links:
chains, necklaces

Business:
corporations, offices, working, desks, staples, papers, typing, printing

The small pocketknife might make you think of:

Weapons:
sharp objects, swords, epees, daggers, warriors

Office implements:
letter openers, box cutters

Things you pare or cut:
wood, apples, pencil points

Being prepared:
scouts, survival, tool kit, first aid

Folded:
portable, hidden, multifaceted

Characters:
Edward Scissorhands, robots, Captain Hook, pirates, monsters

Professionals:
knife throwers, survival shows, army surplus

After making a list of what your objects' attributes cause you to leap to, write a short story using your ideas. Remember you can use the objects as what they actually are, as well as for the concepts they brought to mind. When you're done, go back and notice all the places in your story where your ideas caused the story to go in a particular direction. Think about how you might have used the objects to create a totally different story. Creating a story no one will see allows you to be creative without being judged. Practice giving yourself permission to leap in ways, which might ordinarily feel ridiculous. Notice how useful even the oddest leaps can sometimes be. This activity will contain even more leaping if you do it with another person you can be ridiculous in front of comfortably.

Notes:

Divide to multiply.

Until you become capable of rapidly honing in on what will satisfy the needs of your creative pursuit, you will need to practice consciously noticing more of the available possibilities. Eventually your mind will process these multiple possibilities so rapidly, you might not even be conscious of what you've considered and discarded before landing on what seems like a perfect or nearly perfect fit. In order to use your initial thoughts to generate additional ideas you will need to be multi-conceptual in your approach – record your ideas in a visual manner that allows for eventual manipulation and follow an organic or a systematic process, or a mixed version of these, to make your ideas multiply virally. Let's start with the mindset that will help you to be multi-conceptual in your approach.

Be promiscuous in your generation.

Connect to more than one concept as you generate ideas. Start by thinking of the logical, obvious ideas that usually come to mind first. Remember the rubber washer example; don't judge anything as too boring or predictable. Help yourself to get past any media-influenced thoughts and the other auto-responses most of us have, such as rhyming words and opposites, by recording them quickly. Don't worry whether or not any of your ideas are *the* idea; simply get as many ideas as you can from your mind to your recording mechanism. Follow whatever directions arise. Go with each direction until it feels like a dead end. Imagine that dead end as a cul-de-sac that enables you to quickly turn around and head out to meet another idea by taking your thoughts in a different direction. Generate ideas in as many different areas as you can. Leap before you look, then land and generate additional ideas in that spot. Then leap to another landing spot and do the same thing there. Don't let yourself stay anywhere long enough to get frustrated. Just keep going. Let's use an example to explore this method, but first a quick note about recording your ideas.

Record your ideas.

Record what you think of quickly. Don't let the recording process bog you down. You need to be able to comfortably spew ideas without getting distracted. Pausing can sometimes interrupt your flow. Type or write if you can do it fast enough to keep up fairly well with your thought process. Smart Boards can also be helpful. If a group brainstorms together, one person, who isn't part of the group's idea generating process, can be selected to capture ideas. Another possible method is to have two or three people write down ideas on a white board or large chart *everyone can see*. The back-up coverage this creates allows the recorders to be free to also contribute their ideas. Multiple recorders can help to ensure that fewer ideas end up lost.

Now, let's explore how to take your idea generation to a truly viral place. We all want to think up as many ideas as we can in order to eventually discover *the* idea. This process will enable you to come up with more ideas than you believe you can. It will take you beyond the *I can't think of anything else* place we all get to eventually. Sometimes it takes us quite a while to hit that wall. Other times it seems to pop up out of nowhere and taunt us. We just can't seem to push past it. This process will take you beyond the wall every time. Think of it as breaking through to the other side – the side where the good stuff is often hiding. Now here's a specific idea generating task as an example. First we will explore the auto-responses likely to come to mind almost effortlessly; then we'll walk through the steps of the *divide to multiply* process as it relates to this example.

Use auto-responses as starting points.

Let's imagine you've been given the task to think of all the different ways someone could use a pencil. For the purpose of this exercise we won't consider *why* you've been given this task. We'll simply focus on doing it well. So what *can* you do with a pencil? If you were to jot down your first ideas without judging them, they might be somewhat similar to the list below. The ideas on this list are ones many people often think of rather quickly when given this exercise. You'll notice the list includes quite a few auto-response types of entries.

The pencil sorting example

Here's the initial list:

- write
- draw
- erase

- shade
- tap out a rhythm
- throw it at someone
- twirl it
- stab someone to defend yourself
- use two as chopsticks
- scratch an itch
- gnaw on it when you're nervous
- hold up long hair with it
- save your place in a book
- use as kindling
- key in a phone number or password

Let's pretend you've just finished writing this list and you feel more or less tapped out for the moment. Sorting can now help you to generate more ideas. Keep in mind that the more ideas you start with, the better this method works. It will however, also work with a small group of *starter* items such as the list above.

Use labels intentionally.

Now let's look at our list of 15 ideas and label the concept behind each one. These labels will help you generate more ideas by leading you in different creative directions. We'll start by connecting each idea to a *verb* or *verb phrase*, which represents a concept behind the action. The concept labels listed below are only one set of possibilities. There is no right or wrong label for each word. The labels simply need to make sense to the person generating the ideas.

1) write = *communicate*
2) draw = *make art*

3) erase = *remove something*

4) shade = *make art*

5) tap out a rhythm = *make music*

6) throw it at someone = *hit someone*

7) twirl it = *perform*

8) stab someone = *hurt someone*

9) use two as chopsticks = *pick up food*

10) scratch an itch = *reach something*

11) gnaw on it when you're nervous = *calm yourself*

12) hold your hair up with it = *adorn yourself*

13) save your place in a book = *separate pages*

14) use as kindling = *start a fire*

15) key in a phone number or password = *reach something*

Now, let's add a second label describing the *physical motion* involved in each of the original ideas:

1) write = *communicate + drag*

2) draw = *make art + drag*

3) erase = *remove something + rub*

4) shade = *make art + drag*

5) tap out a rhythm = *make music + tap*

6) throw it at someone = *hit someone + toss*

7) twirl it = *perform + twist*

8) stab someone = *hurt someone + poke*

9) use two as chopsticks = *pick up food + pinch / scissor*

10) scratch an itch = *reach something + rub*

11) gnaw on it when you're nervous = *calm yourself + deface*

12) hold your hair up with it = *adorn yourself + poke*

13) save your place in a book = *separate pages + lay between*
14) use as kindling = *start a fire + destroy*
15) key in a phone number or password = *reach something + tap*

Finally, we'll add a label, which represents the *arena* or *topical area* where each of these actions occurs:

1) write = *communicate + drag + writing*
2) draw = *make art + drag + art*
3) erase = *remove something + rub + writing*
4) shade = *make art + drag + art*
5) tap out a rhythm = *make music + tap + music*
6) throw it at someone = *hit someone + toss + play*
7) twirl it = *perform + twist + play*
8) stab someone = *hurt someone + poke + weapons*
9) use two as chopsticks = *pick up food + pinch / scissor + food / eating*
10) scratch an itch = *reach something + rub + self care*
11) gnaw on it when you're nervous = *calm yourself + deface + self care*
12) hold your hair up with it = *adorn yourself + poke + fashion*
13) save your place in a book = *separate pages + lay between + boundary making*
14) use as kindling = *start a fire + destroy + fuel / raw material*
15) key in a phone number or password = *reach something + tap + communication*

Sort and re-sort to generate more.

Now, we'll explore some of the labels we've created on our list to try to generate other ideas that might also *fit* with them. First we'll approach this task in an organic, leaping fashion and then in a more systematic, logical manner.

The organic, leaping approach begins by selecting two ideas that both have one label in common and then extrapolating to other ideas, which seem to fit into this labeled category. Then it's all freeform leaping from any connection generated that particularly catches our interest to whatever else that connection brings to mind. Below is how the beginning portion of one possible idea generation session using an organic, leaping process might progress:

Both throwing the pencil at someone (#6) and twirling it (#7) are in the *play* category. How else might you *play* with a pencil? You could throw it at a target to earn different amounts of points based on where it landed or have a contest to see who can throw it the farthest. Notice that these ideas are also about the action of *throwing* the pencil. But perhaps instead of focusing on *throwing*, you think of pretending to sword fight with pencils. This of course makes us notice (#8) stabbing someone, which is using the pencil as a *weapon*, similar to using it as a play sword. You can make a spear out of a pencil by attaching it to a shaft. Spears are usually thrown a decent distance. You could throw one to get someone's attention. This is another form of *communicating*, just like (#15) tapping in a phone number to call or text someone. It's a short leap to Morse Code when you mention *tapping* and *communicating* at the same time. This also makes us notice (#5) tap out a rhythm, which is *making music*. How else might you use a pencil to *make music?* You could rub one pencil up and down another one or roll two of them together in your hand to make a clinking noise. You might use the pencil as a mallet to hit something gong-like. Rolling might make you think about *art* again and rolling clay or scoring lines into clay. Rolling clay might make us think of (#9) using two pencils as chopsticks, which makes us think of *food* and *rolling* dough. How else might you use a pencil relative to *food*? You could stab your food instead of picking it up in a chopstick fashion. You could use the pencil to make shish kebob or to roast marshmallows. This makes us think of (#14) use as *kindling*, which makes us think of *burning* the pencil. This takes us back to *communicating* and sending signals at night by waving burning pencils or perhaps using a burning pencil to light a pilot light on a gas stove if we leap back to *food* and *cooking*. This stream of leaping from concepts to motions to topical areas in and among our list of 15 ideas could go on and on and on. But let's stop for now and see how many *extra* ideas we've generated so far. There are 16 of them:

1) throw it at a target for different amounts of points based on where it lands

2) have a contest to see who can throw it the farthest

3) play at sword fighting

4) make a spear out of a pencil by attaching it to a shaft

5) throw to get someone's attention

6) tap out Morse Code

7) rub one pencil up and down another one to make a sound (musical instrument)

8) roll two pencils together in your hand to make a sound (musical instrument)

9) use as a mallet to hit something gong-like

10) roll clay

11) score lines into clay

12) stab your food (eating utensil)

13) use to make shish kebob

14) use to roast marshmallows

15) send signals at night by waving burning pencils

16) use a burning pencil to light a pilot light

Now, let's do the same process using a systematic, logical approach. Once again, there are many ways to do this. The labels you choose to explore first will determine the direction your thoughts and experiences take you.

Below is one version of how the steps of this process might look at the start of a systematic idea generation session:

> Just as we did with the organic process described above, we begin with ideas that have a label in common, but this time we'll include all the entries that share this label. If we choose the *make art* label, ironically, there are only two: (#2) draw and (#4) shade, with this label. We'll list these two idea entries in a category labeled *make art*; if there had been five entries that shared this label, we would have listed them all.

The make art label:

- draw
- shade

Next, we'll ask ourselves the same *how else* question we used as a leaping mechanism in the organic process. *How else could you use a pencil to make art?* As we think of additional ideas, we will add them to our *make art* category list:

The make art list:

- draw
- shade

- roll clay
- build a sculpture out of many pencils
- use the point to poke holes in paper or some other substance to make a pattern
- use the pencil point to make designs in clay
- dip the eraser end in paint and make a pointillism type of painting
- drag the side of the pencil through paint to make sweeping patterns
- glue things to the pencil and wrap things around it to make it decorative
- make a doll or human figure out of it
- lay the pencil on its side and hang things from it to make a mobile

You can see that the organic, leaping process is alive and well within our systematic, logical approach. Let's consider what might have driven the creative leaping journey above.

Shading uses the *side* of the pencil point, and rolling clay uses the pencil on its *side*. Both of these might make you think of the pencil in several *different positions*. This could lead you to think of building a sculpture by placing pencils in *purposeful positions*. You might think of using the point of the pencil to make designs in clay because *clay* from *rolling clay* is still on your mind. The *point* might make you think subconsciously of *pointillism* since we are in the *make art* category, after all. The eraser might seem like a better surface to *dip in paint* than the point. Now that you're thinking of *paint*, you might start to wonder how else you could use a pencil to *apply paint*. Perhaps rolling the clay comes back to mind and suddenly you're visualizing *dragging* the side of the pencil through paint. Then you might leap to doing something *to the pencil* instead of using it to do something to something else. *Attaching* things to the pencil to change its appearance might come to mind. This could lead naturally to doing something *more purposeful and specific* to the pencil instead of decorating it in an abstract fashion. The pencil is a sort of stick. Sticks might make you think of *stick figures* and suddenly you can visualize the pencil being made into a doll. Finally, you might think of *adding things* to the pencil in a different way – tying items to it so that they hang down, which brings you to a mobile. We stopped here, but you could continue. You can also return to this newly generated list (the *make art* list) whenever an entry in another list makes you think of something that would also fit on the *make art* list.

The next step would be to systematically repeat this process for each of the concept labels in our original list of 15 idea entries:

Step 1: Choose one concept label from the original list.

Step 2: Make a new list that includes all the original idea entries that share this same concept label, even if there is only one entry with that label.

Step 3: Ask the *how else* question and generate additional ideas using the organic, leaping process within the confines of the chosen concept label.

Step 4: Add all new ideas that arise to the concept label list.

Once you've finished this process with all the concept labels, repeat it for the motion labels. Pick one motion label and list all the original entries that share that label. Then go back through your newly generated entries in the label lists you've created, such as the ones in the *make art* list, and see which of these also use the same motion as the first motion label you've selected. You might select *poke* as the first label to be considered. Poking holes in paper or another substance to make art would be added to the poke category. After you've added all the new entries that share this motion, it's time to ask a question, only this time it's, *what else?* instead of *how else?* Ask yourself, *What else can I do with a pencil when I poke it?* Perhaps you'll think of poking holes in dirt to plant seeds or to aerate your lawn. You might even think of poking the pencil into the holder on a rural mailbox to replace a broken *please pick up the mail* flag.

Go beyond initial connections.

The final step in the systematic process is to see if any of the entries fit together to form a new list. For example, you might have *toast marshmallows* on a *stabbing* or *food* list, and *burn in a fire* on a *destroy* list. These two could be moved to a *camping* list. Then ask, *How else could a pencil be used when camping?* Here are a few ideas that might occur to you:

- stake a tent
- stab food to remove it from a fire
- hang the toilet paper roll
- mark a trail back to camp by shoving them into the ground along your path
- make a spear to fish
- hammer into a tree to make a hook to hang your pack

We'll stop there, but if you continued to explore different aspects of camping you could generate even more ways to use a pencil. You can also peruse the labels in your original list of ideas to check for any that have not been included in the lists you've generated so far. Perhaps you've used *lay between* but haven't used *boundary making.* You can then generate ideas for ways to use pencils to create boundaries within different contexts.

You can see that this process works really well with the pencil usage example, but how helpful will it be in your creative work and everyday life? It's directly applicable to coming up with ideas in workplace settings. Simply sort your ideas and label them, then use the attributes of each label to help you generate more ideas. Let's look at a real life application that helps to demonstrate how useful this process can be in helping you to see what you might otherwise miss.

Real life example:

Imagine you are making a list of people to invite to a party and you want to make sure you don't forget anyone. If we consider an exaggerated instance of this real life occurrence, it's easy to see how *divide to multiply* would be helpful. Imagine you have been given an enormous amount of money to have a giant gala party. You can invite as many people as you would like. The party will be lavish and enjoyable so you don't want to forget anyone. You sit down and begin to make a list of the people you want to invite. You're nervous you might forget someone. You'd hate to imagine someone finding out about this amazing bash after the event was over and then becoming angry at you for not inviting them. You decide to label the people you plan to invite. Your labels might look something like this:

- family
- people at work
- neighbors
- people I grew up with
- people I went to college with
- people from where I used to live
- my significant other's family
- people who have moved away

- people who are friends with me and my significant other
- people who are friends only with me
- people who came to my wedding
- old friends
- new friends
- people from past relationships I'm still friendly with
- people from my old job
- old friends of my family

As you come up with each label, it becomes a category. You then can think of all the people you know who fall into each category. You'll have a much better chance of not missing anyone if you do this.

Don't stop now.

What else can you notice about the people on your list? What other leaps can you make within your categories? You might realize you've gone on vacations with two or three people from different categories. This creates a new category. This new category makes you think of other categories based on what you *do* with people such as being in the same club or playing a sport together. This might make you think of the people you usually see in a particular context such as your yoga instructor, who is becoming a friend.

Intentionally sorting and re-sorting your ideas into specific conceptual categories can help you to see what you've thought of and what's still out there that fits into one of your categories. It can also help you to think of additional categories. This process helps you to explore in a much more divergent manner and utilizes both the seeing skills presented in Chapter 1 and the leaping process discussed in Chapter 2. Remember to always ask yourself, *how else?* or, *what else?* as you go through this process.

There is no wrong way to *divide to multiply*. The beauty of the process is that it will be unique to your life experiences and knowledge base, because this is what will inform your choices. This is why two or more people doing this process generate even more ideas. You can work together or work separately and then combine your efforts. If you do the process separately, be sure to then resort using all of each other's entries, not just your own. No matter how you choose to *divide to multiply*, the process will help you to generate a lot more ideas, which will give you a far greater chance of finding something useful. Thinking conceptually is the key to the *divide to multiply* process. Noticing the traits and attributes of your ideas will help you to leap to other similar yet different ideas that share these characteristics. This brings us to the Second *See* Key Principle:

Notice conceptual connections.

Over time, with practice, you can learn to use these kinds of conceptual connections to help you to locate an idea, which when developed will become an amazing *fit* for your particular creative pursuit. Some people are capable of doing this process without recording much at all. They do most of the work in their heads. Other people, the luckiest or most skilled, will eventually do this at lightning speed. They'll be able to whiz through categories, leaping without being consciously aware of all the steps their brains are firing through. It almost feels as if they magically *land* on the perfect idea. There are a small number of people who do all of this intuitively. Don't waste too much time envying them. Choose to use your time to *divide to multiply* instead, so you too can generate amazing ideas.

EXERCISES
to help you generate more ideas

Exercise 1:
Create alternate arenas for everyday objects

For each of the following items, think of five other arenas, other than the most obvious one, in which you could also use it. Let's use *pudding* as an example:

You usually eat pudding so it is in the *food* arena.

You could also:

- let children finger paint with it on a tray. It would then be in the *art* arena.
- use it as mortar between bricks. It would then be in the *construction* arena.
- use it to fill a water bed. It would then be in the *furniture* arena.
- fill a very large Ziploc® bag to make a pillow. It would then be in the *bedding* arena.
- use it in a play to represent human waste. It would then be in the *props* arena.

Do this same exercise for the following five items:

- a paperclip
- a large dill pickle
- a man's large white handkerchief

- a fork
- a baseball hat

(Also take note of all the different kinds of motions you use.)

Exercise 2:
Repurpose using an object's original motion

For each of the five objects listed below, come up with three additional ways to use each maintaining the same motion that is used during its original function. Let's use a *rollerblade* as an example:

- A rollerblade rolls with the wheels in contact with a surface. Usually you skate to move yourself from one area to another for transportation, exercise, enjoyment, or a combination of these.

You could also:

- roll the wheels in paint to make lines on a road or other surface
- put your hand inside the skate and roll it over someone's back to massage them
- roll back and forth over nuts in a Ziploc® bag to crush them

Do this same exercise for the following five items:

- a hula-hoop skipping, painting a circu,
- a hammer - photo prop, crush food,
- a flyswatter
- a comb
- a colander or strainer

(Notice all the arenas you use.)

Exercise 3:
Create a gala party list

Create your own party list. Group your invitees into categories. Use category labels to help you think of people you missed. Add any additional people you think to invite into the appropriate categories. Peruse your lists and see if any of the people in various categories have something in common. Create a new category labeled with this shared trait. Generate additional people to place in this new category.

Exercise 4:
The paper cup exercise

Do the pencil exercise described in this chapter, but this time, use a paper cup. Decide if you want to do the organic or the systematic method. Remember to consider what the cup is made of, its shape, and any other characteristics, which will help you to generate ideas. Go through all the steps in the pencil exercise:

- Generate an initial list.
- Give each entry a label based on its action verb.
- Give each entry a label based on the motion used.
- Give each entry a label based on its topical area or arena.
- Notice which entries share labels.
- Use either the organic or systematic generating process described above.

(Notice the connections and leaps you make.)

Organic Process:

Step 1: Choose two ideas from your list that share a label.

Step 2: Ask the *How else* question and extrapolate to additional ideas using the organic, leaping process within the concepts represented by the label you've chosen, but allow yourself to leap to any other category that arises.

Step 3: Record all of your new ideas.

Step 4: Repeat this process by starting with two other ideas that share a label on your list.

Systematic Process:

Step 1: Choose a *concept* label from your list.

Step 2: Put all the original idea entries with this *concept* label into a new list, even if there is only one entry that has the label you've selected.

Step 3: Ask the *How else* question and generate additional ideas using the organic, leaping process within the confines of the chosen label.

Step 4: Add all the new ideas to the new list.

Step 5: Create a new list for each of the other *concept* labels on the original idea list and repeat the above process.

Step 6: Repeat this process for the *motion* labels on your list using the *What else* question.

Step 7: Peruse your concept categories for entries that share the same motion.

Step 8: Peruse all entries to find entries that share a trait not yet labeled.

Step 9: Create and name a brand new list of ideas based on these similarities.

Step 10: Ask the *How else* question to generate more entries for this new list.

Notes:

Plug into your inner crockpot.

Did you ever walk somewhere lost in thought and suddenly look up amazed you hadn't tripped over or run into something because it seemed as if you were paying absolutely no attention to your surroundings? Or perhaps you've driven somewhere only to realize you were on autopilot because you couldn't remember any of the particulars from the last several minutes? Our brains are amazing; they do a lot of work *without us*. This is especially true of the mental gymnastics involved in the process of creation.

Back burner thinking

Think of your brain as having a busy workshop filled with small workers who zip around sifting through all the available pieces of data attempting to locate what might satisfy your current creative needs. These workers sometimes seem to accomplish more when we aren't focusing on what they are doing. Our subconscious also appears to work within a completely different sense of time than our conscious mind. One moment it is performing a viscous, slow motion evolution, and the next, engaging in a time-lapse eruption of discovery.

A quick word about intuition

Intuition doesn't follow a given formula. It takes place when our subconscious makes lightning-speed connections among the enormous amount of stored data our conscious mind might not currently be considering. Our conscious mind is often invested in telling us what *must* or *should* be. It will define something as *right* based on a particular paradigm or preconceived expectation. Our subconscious mind is more like our dream state – it allows us to make conceptual leaps that *feel* right or, at the very least, carry a hint of potential promise. Our logical conscious mind is usually so sure it's right, it scoffs at what it perceives as intuition's apparent lack of validity and often succeeds in silencing or dismissing many of the messages sent to us from our subconscious.

Intentionally seed your thought process.

Directing your subconscious can help it to germinate viable ideas. Questions work really well to guide your subconscious toward what you are seeking. Ask yourself what you need in order to satisfy your project or to solve your problem. Define your need conceptually. Perhaps you need something to convince a new audience to choose to do something or to think a certain way. Your question might start out as: *How can I convince (insert particular group or individual) to do (insert specific action)?* Try rephrasing your original question in a more conceptual fashion. Keep rephrasing your question until the concept behind it becomes more graspable to you, and therefore, to your subconscious. Here are a few examples of how the original question above might be rephrased:

- *What aspects of what I want my audience to do already appeal to them?*

- *What aspects of what I want my audience to do are similar to other things that already appeal to them?*

- *What do I know about my audience's experience with what I am trying to convince them to do?*

- *What is the obvious benefit for my audience if they do what I am trying to convince them to do?*

- *What other benefit might my audience end up with if they do what I am trying to convince them to do?*

- *Who might my audience trust more or listen to more easily than me about what I am trying to convince them to do? Why would my audience be more likely to believe this person or group than me?*

- *Why might my audience resist or reject doing what I am trying to convince them to do?*

- *What are my primary motives for trying to convince my audience to do what I want them to do? Are there any other motives besides the primary ones? Are they equally or less important?*

Keep your logical brain occupied while your subconscious works for you.

Once you've come up with your question, ask it. You may choose to write it or type it. Writing your question down and reading it aloud gives its meaning an additional opportunity to sink in. Then, butt out and let your subconscious, intuitive brain go to work. Seriously, don't try to help your brain at this point. In fact, find something to keep your logical, conscious brain busy so it doesn't bother all those hardworking, intuitive data miners. Go watch a movie, run, paint, read a really good book or something online, do errands, repair something. Do anything that shuts up your logical brain's desire to fix, solve, or produce NOW! It doesn't matter what you choose to do as long as it takes your focus away from the inner subconscious task at hand. Trust the process. You may need to slow down to take your mind off of your question. Your successful *separate-yourself* process might be very zen. Or you might find yourself full of nervous energy and need to do something physical or mentally complicated to keep your inner eyes off of the initial stages of this process. You may need to try several things before you find what works best. Don't be concerned about how others do this. Discover how *you* can do it successfully.

If we: 1) familiarize ourselves with the conditions and aspects of a given situation; 2) frame our need conceptually; and then 3) step out of our own way in order to give our subconscious the space and time to work, then it will usually execute a series of conceptual leaps, which will lead to helpful discoveries. These discoveries will often either end up being what we actually need or will bring us closer to it.

There is usually more than one *good* solution to any creative project; however, those based on initial work done by the subconscious are often more original than those created through methods that only utilize logical thinking, no matter how much divergent thinking is involved in those processes. This is because even when you leap in many directions, if you only leap toward the expected, you can miss finding something that is both unexpected and useful in a truly elegant way.

Be more than one person all by yourself.

I once read a wonderful saying from some Eastern spiritual tradition (I don't remember which one) which postulates that we become a different person when we finish uttering a sentence, any sentence, simply because we have uttered it. Everything we experience has an impact on us. Everything alters our perceptions and thought pathways even if we aren't conscious of it as it occurs, even if it's only by a very small degree. All these small changes add up and cause larger changes over time. Sometimes we intentionally choose how strongly we continue to retain and focus on the memories of specific life experiences. Other times we can't seem to get rid of certain memories no matter how hard we try, or we may find ourselves regretting that we haven't focused more strongly or more often on certain aspects of our past. But all of these life experiences help us to continue to grow and change. It is almost as if we become a different person from moment to moment. What does this have to do with creativity? The *new* person you've become can collaborate with the person you were a few minutes or a few days ago. It's as if you get to put your head together with yourself. You'll now have more than one brain working on your creative task, even though both of the brains are yours. One is your brain – in the state it was in when you started the work, and the other is the brain you have now – the one that has changed due to what you have experienced since you last worked on your project.

Pause and set your work aside.

This *dual brain* advantage is why it's so helpful to pause and put your work aside from time to time. You will return to the work with fresh eyes and a brain altered by new experiences. Most writers know the benefits of putting their work aside and reviewing it a bit later. When they return to what they have written they are able to see what they missed before, things such as: all the obvious holes in their thinking their brains had automatically filled and obscured; new connections that had not originally occurred to them; and smoother transitions between the ideas being conveyed.

Working as part of a creative team brings many more brains and perspectives to the table. This obviously requires you to be receptive to the thoughts of others. (More about this in Chapter 8.) However, even when you are not part of a team, you need to consciously choose to consider and be receptive to what your recently life-altered brain tells you. More importantly, you need to intentionally ask it what it thinks of what you've done so far. You'll risk discovering and having to acknowledge possible boring or confusing aspects of your work; however, you'll also open yourself up to raising the quality not only of specific portions of your project but of its overall impact as well.

Real life example:

I often do crossword puzzles when I have excess conscious energy and want somewhere to *put it* so it doesn't hamper whatever I'm about to do next. One day I was sitting and doing a crossword puzzle from our town's weekly paper. These puzzles are not that difficult. Most of the clues are easy to answer, but there are always two to four that can be a bit tricky. I'm much better at the creatively twisted clues, the ones that require me to think in an unexpected manner, than I am at calling up historical or even celebrity names from memory. That afternoon I had filled in the entire puzzle except for two words, which crossed. Both had creatively twisted clues, but I just couldn't seem to solve them. I decided to take a break and go grocery shopping to pick up a few things. I had plenty of time before I needed to go to the elementary school to meet my son to walk him home. I put the crossword puzzle aside, got in my car and drove the five blocks to the grocery store in town.

I really liked the grocery store. It was a very cool co-op with many natural and organic foods, and it had amazing produce. My car at the time, I didn't like so much. It was a car I had acquired in a recent divorce. It was a friendly divorce, but my ex-husband had a tendency to make pronouncements based more on how he wanted things to be than on how they actually were. His description of the car was one of these wishful pronouncements. It had been his mother's car. She was a little old lady who only drove it to church on Sunday and to volunteer at the local elementary school back in her home state. My ex assured me his mother had taken very good care of the car and had kept up with all the recommended maintenance. The car was a total dud. It was a Saab, which was great for my snowy New England state, but one day, it just decided to come to a stop as I was driving it in town. The motor made a run-dun-dun kind of noise and there was simply no power. I took it to a mechanic. It wasn't the battery or the transmission. He assured me it was some dirt under some cap whose purpose was a total mystery to me. I drove it home. It worked! For a week. Then it repeated its run-dun-dun performance. This time the mechanic told me it was some little part that needed to be replaced. He replaced it. I drove the car home. It worked, this time for two weeks. It happened again. I took it to a different mechanic. He said it was a faulty connection, which of course he fixed. I drove it home. It continued to work well. Three weeks later as I was leaving the grocery store on the day I had set the crossword puzzle aside, the car run-dun-dunned itself to a complete stop once more. I ended up having the car towed. (I eventually sold it to a Saab mechanic.) I walked home with my two bags of groceries, put my purchases away, and carried the crossword puzzle to the table. I sat down, picked up a pencil, said, *Oh yeah* and wrote in the answers to the two clues I just couldn't seem to think of earlier.

Was my unconscious brain working on those clues while I was shopping and dealing with car issues? Probably. Did I think of new connections when I re-approached the puzzle because of not being stuck in my previous train of thought? Also very likely. Did I make new connections in my mind because I had now had new, additional experiences? Perhaps. All I know is that the person who went shopping and had car troubles was much better at finishing that puzzle than the one who had tried to do it earlier.

Bring subconscious simmerings to the surface.

So, how can you bring these newly acquired subconscious thoughts and ideas to the surface? If we continue the metaphor of you being two people, then one of them has to be quiet and listen so the other one can talk. You need to listen to yourself but not just to the self you were yesterday or ten minutes ago. It's no accident that stereotypical mad-but-brilliant-professor or evil genius characters always seem to be talking to themselves. They know how important and valuable what they have to say to themselves is. Certain people might think you're a touch crazy if they hear you talking to yourself, but actually, you'll be more brilliantly in touch with the inner workings of your thought process than many people who seem saner by virtue of their refusal to talk to themselves.

Observe what comes up in your mind once you've returned to your set-aside project. Leap in whatever directions your intuition tells you to go. Remember intuition is your brain making leaps at the subconscious level based on the connections it perceives, which in turn are based on the past experiences which it chooses to focus on. Trust the process but judge the hell out of your choices as you go. Creating successfully means making choices that *fit* your needs in elegant and perhaps unexpected ways, but no matter how original your ideas or designs are, they are no good at all if they do not work for the particular needs of your current project.

Neuron-string-based bursts of thought can feel like magic.

Sometimes, after you set aside your work and then return to it, you have such a fully formed, outrageously perfect, and unique thought, it feels as if it has landed magically in your lap. This is the payoff for trusting your subconscious to choose which leaps may be the best. It is also a product of your willingness to hand over some of the initial judging-to-see-if-it-fits-your-needs decisions to your subconscious, thus allowing more fully formed and vetted ideas to rise directly to the surface where they become available to your conscious mind. When this happens we all do a happy dance. Then we take the time to notice what led up to this magical moment. It might not be the same for you as it is for someone else who is just as creative as you. It doesn't matter. Just notice what happened. Record it. Repeat it. Then try like hell to make it happen again.

Trust your intuition.

Be willing to leap to those places your intuition pushes you toward. Leap before you look as you trust the direction in which your subconscious leads you. However, once you land, be sure to look around and judge whether you've arrived at your final destination or are simply a step closer to getting there. Also judge whether what you would be able to produce from the ideas forced to the surface by your subconscious, would fit your current creative needs practically and artfully in an enticing and interesting way. But don't be too quick to judge. Give your subconscious the benefit of the doubt. Slow down and take in what it tells you. Trust that your inner subconscious thought-process is more similar to a roomful of enlightened beings than a roomful of monkeys. Your subconscious might chatter just as much as a bunch of hairy simians, but once you learn to trust and decode its messages, it'll start using a loudly beeping, oversized neon arrow you can't miss to point you toward a productive creative path.

EXERCISES
to help you use your back burner

Exercise 1 Version 1:
Question without questing – using a small practical task

Find a small task you want to accomplish in your home or office. Let's imagine you've decided you want to figure out where all your spending cash goes so quickly. There are lots of ways out there to track what you spend your money on each day. Some of them are clunky or obtrusive, and others work well for some people but may not be ideal for you. Let's assume you want to come up with your own method. First you'll need to figure out exactly what it is you want to track. Maybe you want to know how long the cash in your wallet lasts. Or perhaps you want to know how much cash you spend on coffee and snacks. Define what you want to discover. Write down this goal statement and fill in the blank:

I want to discover _____ *each week.*

A few possible examples:

I want to discover:

- how much cash I take out of the ATM each week.
- how much money I spend on coffee (not at mealtimes) each week.
- the average amount of money I spend on non-essentials each month.
- how little I can spend on extras each week without feeling deprived.

Once you've decided what it is you want to discover and have written your statement, read it and then put it aside. Look at it again before you go to sleep that night. Read it in the morning when you get up. Then forget about it. If you start to think about it, notice your thought, complete your thought, and then let it go. Stop focusing on your goal statement. When you get home, take out your statement, read it, and then write anything and everything that occurs to you in that moment, including what you remember thinking during the day. Freewrite without judgment. Don't edit. This is another moment when talking to yourself out loud can really help. Don't be shy. Try it. If it helps, do it. If it doesn't help you, stop doing it, but you won't know until you try. Read what you have written and see if it makes you think of a system of actions to take to help you discover what you have expressed in your goal statement.

What happened when you did this? Did you find yourself having more ideas than you thought you would? If not, it might be because this example isn't one you were very invested in at the present moment. It could also be because your statement could do with a little refinement to make it more specific. Make a mental note of what happened during this experience and why you think it happened that way for you.

Exercise 1 Version 2:
Question without questing – using a larger aspirational task

Try this again with a larger project. Something you truly aspire to make happen in your life. Go through the same steps. This is especially effective if you do it with a partner. Find a common change you'd like to create in your lives. Do the exercise separately. When you are done, share your ideas with each other and then use the additional ideas you acquired from each other to help you think of even more possibilities. Make sure you give yourselves the back-burner time you need. Be sure to not think about your project or task until the time you've set aside to let the ideas on each of your respective back burners spill into your consciousness.

Exercise 2:
Name retrieval roundabout

Next time you can't remember something, perhaps an actor's name, or the name of a restaurant, book, or movie, write a really simple question such as, *What was the name of the restaurant I wanted to tell Bill about?* on a piece of paper and then go and do something else, or talk about something else with Bill. This might be interesting to do while you are talking to Bill on the phone. Try to forget all about the name you are trying to remember. Let's say it's the name of a restaurant you want to recommend to Bill. Don't attempt to recall it. After about five minutes, if the name hasn't spontaneously fallen out of your mouth, look at your question and see if the name comes to you. Try not to think of the name until you read the question again.

If this doesn't work, write or say everything you can remember about the restaurant. Simply say a stream of whatever occurs to you. It doesn't need to be organized or logical. You might talk about the food, the décor, something you noticed someone doing there, a conversation you had there, whatever. Talk about everything and anything except the name and consciously try to avoid putting any of your energy into recalling the name. Then see if the name pops back into your mind.

Exercise 3:
Ten times is a charm

Write a phrase or sentence you would put on a bumper sticker to proclaim and promote your worldview. Don't worry about writing it well. Just write it on the first line of a piece of paper after thinking about it for a few minutes. Then rewrite it right away nine more times. Don't worry about perfecting it; simply try to make it convey your meaning a little more clearly each time. Stop after you've done the tenth edit. Put the paper away. Try not to think about it. (You could also type it on a screen and hit return after each version.)

On the following day, reread your final sentence and then rewrite it five more times. Do it the same way you did the first ten rewrites, one right after the other on the next line. After the fifth rewrite put it away and don't look at it for five days. Take it out on the fifth day and tweak it until you like it.

Did taking a break from your writing help you to *see* it with fresh eyes? Did the time away help you to shift your focus? Notice what happened for you. How might this process be useful in other endeavors?

Exercise 4:
Backburner encounter preparation

You can use a method similar to Exercise 3 to help you prepare for an encounter. Before planning a meeting, presentation, or an important conversation, write a short statement about what you want to achieve during the event. Don't worry about writing it well; simply try to capture in one sentence what you want to achieve. Then put the statement away and prepare the way you normally would for your scheduled encounter. Put your plan aside for a least an hour. Reread your statement just before you review your plan.

Notice if your statement has an impact on how you view and/or edit what you have planned. Read the statement again just before the encounter starts. The back burner thoughts generated by your subconscious when you put your single statement of purpose aside may help you to create a more focused and clear communication.

Exercise 5:
Sweet interruptions

Next time you're having a disagreement with someone, try this. Ask them to humor you and pause for a few moments to talk together about the desserts you each enjoy the most. Take turns rhapsodizing for a few minutes about sweets you love to eat. Discover what you both enjoy and what one or the other of you can't stand. Then say, *Okay, what were we talking about?* You might be surprised to discover that your emotions have cooled down and it suddenly becomes a little easier to find common ground. You can positively sidetrack your own mind in this same manner whenever you get stuck trying to think of an idea or a solution. Stop whatever you are doing and think about desserts you enjoy, places you'd like to visit, or things that have recently made you laugh. If stopping your task makes you anxious, assure yourself that you're going to get back to it in just a few minutes. Meanwhile, push away any thoughts about what you were previously trying to do. After a few minutes, go back to your original undertaking. You will probably feel fresher and better able to tackle your task. At the very least, you'll feel more relaxed, which will help you to focus more clearly.

Notes:

Find it, don't force it.

In order to create something we first need to conceive it. We have to imagine *what* we are trying to create. But this is a bit of a contradiction, because in the beginning we do not have a *specific* vision of what we are attempting to bring into being. Nevertheless, we need to be able to describe it conceptually to ourselves in order to grasp a *sense* of it. Once produced, this conceptual *germ* can help us to recognize which of the myriad of possible component *parts* can be combined and/or tweaked to successfully satisfy the needs of our current creative endeavor.

Being definitive is usually viewed as a positive practice. This is not always the case when we're thinking creatively. Many of us would consider the ability to clearly define the solution we are seeking to be an advantage. However, narrowly defining what we need causes us to reduce the size of our search area. This sounds like a good thing – a smaller area to search seems to imply a faster and easier path to solution. However, if we define what we're looking for too narrowly, it can predetermine the paths we choose as we search for what we need. If our vision is too specifically defined, if we have created an it-has-to-look-like-this picture of what we are hoping to find, we may end up bypassing stellar, amazing solutions in our rush to find what we've predetermined we need. We become far-sighted. We see an image of what we've set as our goal off in the distance and then we run to see how fast we can get there. We're no longer attempting to discover something amazing; instead, we're busily rejecting anything we see along the way that doesn't match what we've already decided we should procure.

Instead of rushing forward toward a preselected destination, we could choose to use critical thinking skills to help us form a conceptual grasp of the needs of our particular creative task. We could then weave our creative task's requirements into a conceptual net to help us to sift through and capture those things that fit into a possible solution in ways we may have been able to predict and also in ways we had not yet begun to imagine. Discovering these unpredictable ways often leads to truly inventive solutions. If we allow ourselves to *conceptualize the needs* of our task, instead of attempting to *narrowly and specifically define what is needed*, we make it easier and more likely for us to discover elements we can merge and connect to satisfy our creative task's needs in innovative and excellent ways.

There was a joke circulating on the internet several years ago. It has popped up again and again intermittently. I used a version of it in my class to demonstrate how choosing not to predetermine what we need in a specific and fixed manner can make room for inventive solutions. The joke goes something like this:

There once was an old man who loved to grow tomatoes. One spring there was a series of intermittent torrential downpours interspersed with hot dry spells. This made the clay soil in the old man's backyard very hard. The old man didn't have the strength to turn the soil for planting. He didn't believe in using machines to do the jobs *a man should do*, and he was too proud to ask anyone but family for help. Unfortunately for the old man, his only remaining family was his grandson Joseph, who was currently spending the final year of his 5-year sentence in the penitentiary about 50 miles away. That week when the old man wrote to his grandson, as he did every Monday, he told him about the condition of the soil. He also told him how disappointed he was not to be able to plant tomatoes that year. He ended his letter with: *Joey, you're such a good boy. I know if you were here that you'd get the garden ready for your old granddad. But you can't be here this year. Such is life. It simply wasn't meant to be. What's most important is that you take good care of yourself, keep your nose clean, and come home to your grandpa who loves you very much. I know you're a good boy, Joey, and that you could never have done what they said you did.*

A few days later, the old man was startled awake in the wee hours of the morning by brisk, loud pounding on his front door. *FBI, open up!* The old man shuffled to the door and asked what was happening. *We have a warrant to search your property, sir,* answered the agent. *Just stay in your house until we give you the all-clear.* The old man heard what sounded like the beep-beep of large trucks or heavy equipment backing up. Later, there was another knock at the door. *You can come out now, sir. We put things back the best we could,* said the agent. The old man walked out as the agent got into the only remaining vehicle and drove away. Most of the backyard had been dug up and refilled. The soil was loose and ready for planting.

The old man smiled. A few days later, the old man received a letter from his grandson: *Dear Granddad, sorry I couldn't be there in person to help you with your tomatoes. Hope everything ended up the way I hoped it would. Love, Joey.* The old man smiled again.

Let's examine the above scenario to see what we can learn from it.

How did the old man's constraints limit his possible solutions?

The old man wasn't willing to use machines to till his soil. This ruled out renting or borrowing a rototilling type of device. He also was only willing to accept help from his family. Since his only living relative was currently locked up in prison, this also was not an option.

What did the old man tell his grandson he knew he would do for him if he were able?

The old man let Joey know that he knew if Joey were home he'd prepare the garden for his grandfather.

How did Joey define what was needed?

Joey obviously did not define his grandfather's need to: have his grandson (Joey, his only remaining family) come home to till the garden for him. If he had, Joey might have chosen to break out of jail. If he were lucky enough to escape without being recaptured he may have been able to make it back to his grandfather's to till the garden, but then what? There were only two possible outcomes if Joey chose to break out of jail: 1) he could get caught; or 2) he could be on the run forever. Either of these two options would break his grandfather's heart, and as his grandfather pointed out, Joey is a good boy and would not want to make his grandfather unhappy.

So how *did* Joey ultimately define what was needed? He probably asked himself what he could do to help his grandfather prepare his garden for planting while still honoring his grandfather's wish for him to stay out of trouble and come home at the end of his sentence. Joey didn't predetermine *who* would do the tilling.

How did Joey's conceptualization of what was needed help him to come up with a solution?

Since Joey needed to serve out his sentence to keep his grandfather happy, he needed to help him from inside the prison. This sounds impossible but Joey was resourceful and a good creative thinker. He knew that if he stayed in prison, someone else had to do the tilling.

Did Joey honor his granddad's constraints?

Since his grandfather wouldn't accept help from a tilling service or from nonfamily members, Joey needed a solution that bypassed these constraints while still honoring them. His grandfather would not accept Joey paying a gardening service to do the work, nor would he want Joey to ask friends or neighbors to do the tilling. So Joey did what he could; he dropped a hint that something might be buried in the backyard. Of course the FBI jumped on it. Of course they checked it out, and in the process, they tilled his grandfather's garden for him. Since Joey's grandfather had no control over what the FBI did, he was willing to accept the results of their actions. Besides, it obviously all transpired because of his smart and helpful grandson.

Joey shows us our goal should be to determine *what* we are trying to accomplish rather than *how* we are going to accomplish it. His story also demonstrates how undesirable side effects – such as a longer prison sentence or being on-the-run – can sometimes occur when people are unwilling to look beyond the first idea that seems to work. This can also happen when an exhausted creative team is relieved to finally find something that satisfies at least the primary needs of their project. Neglecting to completely vet a solution we think is really clever may also produce unexpected negative domino effects. It is good practice to look beyond your first idea, whether it is an instantly favorite idea or an in-a-rush-to-get-it-done idea. Commit to doing some serious digging to discover what you don't know that you don't know. Others can help you by bringing their experience, knowledge, or alternate lenses to the situation.

Sometimes, even in everyday life, we come up with an idea that seems like a really good solution but we don't realize it doesn't satisfy the given need for someone else. Let's look at a hypothetical example. Imagine a friend is visiting you. You are excited to see her and want to show her a good time. She tells you she read an article on a travel site about an ice cream shop in your town that is famous for its unusual flavors. She's especially looking forward to trying their mushroom chocolate even though it sounds disgusting because it received tons of rave reviews on the site. When the two of you get to the shop, there's a sign on the door: *Closed today to repair burst water pipe – reopening tomorrow.* Unfortunately you and your friend have waited until the last full day of her visit to go to the ice cream shop. She's flying out early the next day. You feel badly she missed the ice cream. You begin to suggest other dessert alternatives. Your town has several fabulous bakeries, a couple of cafés with excellent pastries, and frozen yogurt and soft-serve ice cream places. Your friend isn't enticed by any of your suggestions. She decides to pass on dessert. You can tell she's disappointed even though she's not making a big deal about it. You wonder why she hasn't chosen one of the alternatives you've offered. The ice cream she missed was pretty special, but everything else you've suggested is really good too. You begin to feel just the tiniest bit miffed and to think she's being a little too picky. Just then you walk past a cupcake bakery. You hadn't suggested it earlier because it's only a so-so kind of place. Your friend looks in the window and sees a maple bacon cupcake. *Oh my, that's so odd. I simply have to try it,* she exclaims. You grab her arm as she begins to pull open the door and whisper that the place isn't really that great. *That's okay with me,* she says, *I just really wanted to try something new and unusual.*

Now you get it. She wasn't looking for *delicious* she was looking for *different.* The ice cream she originally wanted was both *delicious* and *different;* however, *different* was the most important characteristic as far as your friend was concerned. In fact, for her, it was the driving factor, the one that trumped all the other factors. You assumed deliciousness was the most important thing to her. If it had been, your suggestions would have been perfect. But it wasn't, so they weren't. They fell short. You became frustrated because you knew your suggestions were good. You knew they matched the delicious criterion. Here's what's really interesting: your friend might not have realized why your suggestions didn't appeal to her. She may not have noticed when she read about the ice cream being delicious and unique that she was more interested in the unusual flavors than in the quality of the ice cream. She may have only been conscious of her desire to try the ice cream. Once the ice cream became unavailable, your friend was hoping for an experience to replace the one she was denied. However, since she wasn't aware she was putting more importance on the uniqueness than on the deliciousness of the ice cream, she was unaware of the type of replacement that would satisfy her.

Your replacement suggestions were based on deliciousness, possibly for two reasons: 1) your assumption that this is what your friend was interested in; and 2) your own interest in the deliciousness of desserts. We often superimpose our own assessment criteria when we explore, sometimes intentionally and other times with less awareness. Fortunately for both of you, your friend stumbled upon something that matched her top criterion. As a witness to this occurrence, you became aware of the importance of the uniqueness factor in your friend's craving as she happily purchased and prepared to experience her maple bacon cupcake.

Assuming we already know the most important criteria needed to solve or satisfy a creative endeavor – without first doing a sufficient amount of discovery – can cause us to end up with many excellent ideas that all fit the wrong criteria perfectly. Sometimes we get the criteria wrong because we've made an assumption. Sometimes we superimpose our own values onto a situation. Sometimes the person assigning the creative task does a poor job communicating the criteria that need to be satisfied, or they themselves may not fully understand what is needed. Ironically, even if *we* are the initiator of our creative task, we – just like the ice cream seeking woman in the above example – may be unaware of a particular criterion that is driving us.

So what do you do when you don't really know which concepts are the most important to satisfy for your project? You figure it out as you go. Often when we suggest a movie to go see with a friend, we may assume we know what our friend likes. But what if your friend nixed every movie you suggested? What if their negative responses also didn't seem to have any discernible pattern? You might end up asking your friend if they actually want to go to the movies. If they insist they do, you could help them to figure out what movie they would be interested in seeing. One way to do this would be to continue to make movie suggestions without getting irritated if your friend continues to dislike each movie you suggest. Then ask questions to help them identify *why* the movies you've suggested don't appeal to them. This could then help them to identify what *would* appeal to them. Remember your goal is discovery. Friends, clients, managers, producers, all kinds of people often either don't know what they want, or they have trouble communicating it if they do. Stay focused on your discovery process. Don't take their lack of decisiveness personally. You may have to wade through numerous examples of what they *don't* want as you help them to get closer and closer to realizing what they *do* want.

When your ideas make your stomach hurt

Sometimes a creative idea appears to be absolutely perfect, but it gives you get a weird feeling in your stomach, telling you something about it is not quite right. When this happens, try to discover what that *something* is. One way is to tweak particular aspects of the idea to make them obviously wrong. This can help bring any hidden *wrong* attributes of your seemingly *good* idea to light. Categorize your idea's components. What's there? What does each aspect of your idea contribute? Don't do this in a panicked frenzy. Take your time as if you're crafting something worthy of your effort and attention. Instead of focusing on the possible disaster of not being able to figure it out in time, focus on how rewarding it would be to discover the one *tweak* that would make your idea fabulous and fitting. Fear can diminish our flow of ideas. Too much fear can completely stop our creative flow. Imagine your creative flow in a pipeline with a valve at the end that controls the volume of ideas streaming out of the faucet. Be aware that negativity breeds fear. Fear can bring us back to over-tightened, constricted valves. Take a break if you need to calm your nervousness. Be aware of your self-talk too. The words you say out loud *and* those you think inside have an enormous impact on your process. Chill.

Work on perfecting versus being perfect.

If you expect to locate a shiny and perfect solution to a problem, you risk missing a truly brilliant solution because you may not recognize it when you first encounter it in its partially formed state. You may end up rejecting something before it can show you what it can become. Try to treat each idea that appears to have the possibility of satisfying your project's needs as a potential gem, one you are willing to polish just a little to see if it might shine. I'm not suggesting you waste time doing this with every idea. Rather imagine yourself using a metaphorical net – woven from the major concepts you want your idea to satisfy – to scoop up any potential ideas that appear to fit into it. Over time you will get better and better at recognizing which ideas have the potential with just a few adjustments to become contenders. You'll also get savvier about realizing which ideas will never be viable no matter how much tweaking they receive, and you'll become more adept at letting those ideas pass quickly through your net.

Stress invites you to fall back into old, unhelpful habits.

It's human nature to return to what has worked for us in the past. It's intelligent to learn from our experiences and to repeat behaviors that bring about desired results. However, it is also human nature to stick with a coping mechanism that no longer works. Throwing a tantrum may have worked when we were children, but it probably no longer produces the same results it once did. Even though people may still pay attention to us when we get upset, they are likely to be far less enthusiastic about putting up with unreasonable outbursts now that we are grown-ups. In fact, this formerly effective behavior is much more likely to produce unwelcome results at this stage of our lives.

Old habits are difficult to break. New habits take time to develop into trusted *go-to* responses. When we get stressed or scared most of us go into survival mode. We bring out what passes for our heavy artillery, our big defense shields, or our strongest attack weapons. These often consist of what we've used to protect ourselves in the past – the behaviors we've done for the longest period of time, no matter how ineffective or negative they may be. Instead of destroying our stress or the source of our stress, these behaviors often become weapons of *mass distraction* skewing us away from conscious thought and toward kneejerk, habit-based subconscious reactions. This is the very definition of same-old-same-old. Not a very fertile environment for creativity. If we let the stress of being passionate or terrified about the outcome of a particular creative pursuit overly affect us, we are likely to end up right back in this ineffective automatic response cycle. We may not be aware this is happening. We might not notice our own behaviors, because we are so firmly locked into autopilot. It's as if we've put on blinders, covered our ears, and started chanting *nuh, nuh, nuh, nuh* to keep ourselves from noticing our panic or the poor choices it is encouraging us to make. We tell ourselves, and others, we have the situation well handled as evidenced by all the energy we are channeling toward completing the task at hand. What we don't always notice in these situations is that much of our energy is negative. While it's true that a little fear or worry can positively motivate most of us, fear more often clouds our judgment as we stay in panic mode and forget to think. Everyone panics. It happens all the time. Survivors are those who cycle through their panic quickly and then intentionally begin to start thinking.

Why do so many of us revert to old habits when we fear failure?

Often, when we become afraid, our subconscious kicks into auto-response in an attempt to save us. We don't want to admit that many of these auto-responses, and their accompanying behaviors, are functionally ineffective, because if we do, we'll *really* panic. Why? Because we'll have no idea what to do, and not knowing what to do can invite us to feel alone, powerless, and vulnerable. Many of us are so deeply invested in believing our (ineffective) auto-responses are effective that we'd rather risk crashing and burning in the moment than admit our whole response system might be broken. The irony is that it is extremely difficult to be successful creatively, or in most areas of life, unless we choose to progress past our ineffective auto-responses to stressful situations. But many of us aren't willing to replace them with something potentially – and perhaps even exponentially – better, because we are still convinced we won't succeed without them.

Timing can be everything.

Some times are simply the wrong times. The flow isn't flowing. The resistance seems too much to push past. Other times all you have to do is sit down and begin. The flow dribbles and spurts and then suddenly begins to increase to a steady, dependable volume. If this doesn't happen, then the very idea of picking up your creation once again can feel overwhelming, as if you don't possess the strength to shoulder the weight of your current undertaking. Sometimes this is fear. Sometimes it's part of your process, a respite your subconscious needs to effectively work on your creation without you. Of course it's still *you* doing the work but your conscious mind may not receive the output until hours or days later. Your current resistance to working on your creation may be a useful part of your process or you may be stymied by fear. You can learn when to block out the negative, fearful thoughts and plow ahead, and also when to nurture yourself in other ways as your subconscious is working diligently in the background to advance your endeavor. You may need to experience numerous instances of your subconscious successfully delivering a creative idea or solution to you, after you have left it on its own to work without your conscious mind looking over its shoulder, before you begin to trust this method enough to use it habitually. We humans tend to trust patterns of behaviors more readily than what may appear to be an anomaly.

The amount of time you choose to spend on a creative work session can also affect your process. The duration of one of your sessions may be quite different than that of other creatives. The length of your own sessions may vary from day to day or week to week. There is no *right* or *best* creative session length. Fast processors tend to work intensely and quickly for short bursts of time with large rest periods in-between. However, many of these creative types fill those rest periods with other creative projects and with nurturing and restful activities for their bodies and minds. Other creative individuals crave or need the structure of regularity, choosing to work the same amount of time, at the same time of day, each of their working days. Still others have a creative habit that alternates between these two approaches. Depending on whose advice you listen to, one approach or another is often identified as the definitive best. There is a definitive best for you; it just may not be the same as what's best for someone else. Give yourself permission to do what works for you. Don't waste time attempting to meet an ideal regardless of whether it is externally or internally imposed or suggested.

We often get stuck when we're almost done.

As we get closer and closer to finalizing our creation or solution we can be tempted to fall into one or more common traps that have the potential to crush our creative spark. Some traps do this by spinning us out of control; some immobilize us; some attack our senses and mess with our perception of reality; and others pull us slowly toward despair and surrender.

The Rushing Trap, AKA The race of fear

Sometimes we begin to inexplicably speed up our process. It takes on a careening-down-the-hill velocity we didn't intend, but once this acceleration kicks in, we feel powerless to stop it. We no longer seem to be in charge of the pace of our creative process. It actually feels as if it's speed-dragging us toward the finish line. We begin to believe slowing down will get us trampled. This isn't true. The situation isn't out of our control. We are the one causing it even though the force feels external. Our fear is usually the cause of this runaway train phenomenon. Maybe we fear we will fail. Maybe we fear we'll succeed. Maybe we worry people won't *get it*, that they won't see or understand our work. This can also lead to a second potential trap.

The Compromise Trap, AKA Inner doubts or external pressure

If we doubt the worth of what we have begun to produce for our creative endeavor, we may also begin to question our ability to accurately judge what's good and what's not. We may then choose to alter and adjust our ideas or project in numerous small ways, hoping to forestall the potential negative judgments we fear receiving. Each of these slight but forced alterations may end up diminishing the uniqueness, the shininess, the impact, or even the effectiveness of our creation. The overly sanitized nature of our final product may ensure that it offends almost no one; its bland-ness, however, will undoubtedly cause it to fail to attract or impress anyone. Externally induced doubt can invite us to rework a par-tially finished creation into an unrecognizable construction that no longer satisfies the needs of our original task, even if it does manage to silence some of the insistent naysayers (real or imag-ined) in our immediate vicinity. Welcome critique but trust your-self and your continued assessment of the state of your creation.

The Eternal Tweakage Trap, AKA When you just can't stop

The belief that *just one more* slight alteration will *really make our creation great* can become habit forming. It can pull us into a vortex of never ending tweakage. In a misguided attempt to force our creation into excellence we may find ourselves tweaking one aspect and then another and another and another. We don't seem to know when or how to stop. We usually reach this emotionally frenzied state when we shift our focus so far from the concepts we are trying to embody in our creation that we simply snip and add until we end up with something that looks like a bride with too many bows and an uneven haircut. We mean well. Our intentions are good, but instead of analyzing our creation's current attributes against the requisite conceptual framework of our project, we race frantically toward an idealized and ill-defined version of success. As a result, our sense of *excellence* becomes disconnected from the true purpose of our creative task.

It doesn't matter why you end up doubting yourself, when you do. You may discover that your precious, no matter how tenuous, understanding of what your project needs has somehow inexplicably fallen out of your grasp. You may look up and find it is utterly and completely gone. You may find yourself unable to reconnect to it. This will invite you to begin to doubt yourself even more. Desperation will descend. You will attempt to force-connect disparate concepts within your project in a manic and unhinged quest to reacquire an understanding of what is needed. When this doesn't produce positive results, you will probably panic. Your panic will invite you to continue to make unfortunate choices.

When this happens, step away. Take a breath. Recognize you've left your intuition and your ability to think and *see* in a conceptual manner behind. You have hyper-activated your critical, linear thinking to the point where it now overshadows all other types of thought. The creative dance is over. Plodding, or perhaps marching, has taken its place. In short, something has killed your creative flow. You can't force it to come back. It's staying away because it doesn't like the environment you're in right now. It recognizes hostile territory. It's not stupid. You shouldn't be either.

Breathe. Do whatever you need to do to shake off your fears. It's especially important to at least temporarily separate yourself from anyone who is adding to your confusion. The simple act of focusing on something else for a while often proves to be helpful. Don't worry, your subconscious will stay engaged and come back out to play when you return. Or you may be able to focus on one small aspect of your process, connect with that singular piece, and work your way slowly back to a zone of understanding. Whatever you do, don't try to control what's happening. You can't. You *can* make an inviting playground, a fertile petri dish filled with permission to grow and discover, but you cannot force connections. Connections happen when flying sparks of conceptual inspiration find and ignite each other in elegant ways. Forcing square pegs into triangular holes in painful and awkward ways rarely results in elegance. It does fill up the holes, but it doesn't look good and we all know it.

Don't trip yourself up as you race to the finish line.

Imagine you have come up with an idea or solution for your creative endeavor that is really close to what you need but not quite as good a fit as you had hoped to produce. Your inner voice is likely to start worry-warting comments inside your head: *But we need to put this puppy to bed. It's good enough. Leave it alone.* Or you might convince yourself that what you have created is actually amazing. You may even manage to make your lips say this out loud. Your stomach usually refuses to be fooled. It knows more development is needed. Often, in these situations, it takes only a little more development to take your work from good to spectacular. But you got scared. You worried your work wasn't going to be great, so you stopped. This is the *error-of-omission-isn't-really-failure* theory in action. Over a bazillion advocates of this theory have been served with failure-to-excel judgments. Nonetheless, you managed to convince yourself to stop once your work reached the *reasonably acceptable* mark. You rationalized that you won't be held accountable because you didn't screw it up by trying to develop it further. Is *acceptable* what you were trying to achieve? Did you put your passion, time, and energy into trying to create something acceptable? Really? Come on, who are you kidding? Besides, if you stop at acceptable there is no chance, zip, of ever creating something truly amazing.

EXERCISES
to help you find, not force

Exercise 1:
The bathtub story

Picture a woman in her home getting ready to go on a business trip. She plans to leave for the airport in about 30 or 40 minutes to get there on time for her flight. She has a carry-on bag open on her bed. She's alternating between placing things in the bag and tidying up her house. She detests coming home to a mess. She plans to take a quick bath before she drives to the airport. She can hear the water filling the bathtub. The woman continues to efficiently throw things into her bag, tidy up her home, and keep watch on the level of the tub. When the tub is full, she: turns off the water; throws a belt she almost forgot to pack into her travel bag; scoops up the mail that has accumulated on the rug under the mail slot in the front door; drops the mail into a basket; and returns to the bathroom to take her bath. When the woman tests the temperature of the water she discovers it's way too hot. She turns on the cold water. An odd noise and a burst of air is all that comes out of the faucet. She hears a beep-beep-beep back-up kind of noise from the street. She peeks out around the edge of the curtain on the front window and sees workers and equipment digging up the street further down the block. Unbeknownst to the woman, one of the pieces of mail she didn't open is a notice from the city informing residents about the water main being shut off for a few hours that morning.

How would you define the woman's problem? Write a one-sentence describing what this woman *needs*.

Did you suggest something the woman needs to do to prevent her problem?

If you mentioned that she needs to be more organized or to read her mail in a more timely manner, you are right, but those *needs* define what she could do to *prevent* the problem from happening next time, not to *address* it this time. It's good information she may end up using to avoid a repeat of her current situation, but right now she's standing in front of a bath that's too hot and she needs to leave for the airport soon.

Did you describe what the woman is trying to obtain, or to make happen?

Maybe you said the woman needs: 1) cold water; 2) to lower the temperature of the water in her tub; or 3) to get clean.

Let's explore each of these possible descriptions of what the woman needs.

Obtaining cold water would certainly solve the woman's the-water-is-too-hot-in-the-tub situation. However, defining what the woman needs in this way limits the number of ways she will try to solve her problem. If she doesn't have timely access to cold water, she may believe there's no other way to solve her problem.

Lowering the temperature of the water allows the woman to think beyond adding cold water to the tub. It helps her to *broaden* her search. Perhaps she will think of tossing in ice cubes or packages of frozen peas to cool the water. Things are getting a bit more creative now, but we can still make our description of what the woman needs even more conceptual. Maybe the woman's freezer is broken, or she's all out of ice and the only frozen food she eats is ice cream. Then what?

If we say the woman *needs to get clean*, we create even more possible ways to get her what she needs. Perhaps she could dash into her health club or a friend's house on the way to the airport. She may or may not have time to do this. She could also dip all of her washcloths into the water and use them to give herself a brief but adequate sponge bath.

The woman really wants to be clean when she gets on the airplane, but maybe she doesn't have to be. Maybe she can get clean when she gets to her destination. She may, on the other hand, be meeting clients or someone else important as soon as she steps off the plane. Perhaps the woman needs to look *presentable* for this meeting rather than to be *as clean as she wishes she could be*. Maybe she smells and looks fine already but her hair really needs to be washed. Filling small cups with water and using it to rinse or wash her hair could do the trick. So might a particular hairstyle.

Maybe what the woman really needs is *to arrive at her destination on time and to look presentable when she gets there*. Notice how this description of what the woman needs helps a problem solver to be open to numerous and varied ways to address the situation. The first few narrowly defined sample descriptions of the situation (listed above) decrease the number of possible solutions that would be likely to occur to a problem solver in this situation.

Exercise 2:
The exaggerated & opposite techniques

The next time you attempt to come up with a creative solution, choose one of the ideas you are considering and exaggerate it to the point where it becomes at least partially ridiculous. The solution you concoct does not have to make sense, but it should still satisfy at least one of the needs of your situation. Then take the same original idea but this time morph it so that it becomes functionally opposite in some manner.

Distorting and playing with your solution ideas in these ways can help you to determine how well they address the various needs of your problem situation. For example, recognizing one of the negative consequences that would result if you applied your *exaggerated* solution in real life could reveal a previously unperceived yet vital aspect of the problem your actual solution fails to satisfy. This can help you to determine if you are fixated on only one of your situation's needs and ignoring others. Noticing how certain aspects of an *opposite* solution would fail to work if applied in real life can also help you to identify what your chosen solution may be lacking. Here are two examples to demonstrate how this process works.

Problem Example 1:
Staying dry in the rain

Imagine you just pulled into a parking lot near a long walkway leading to the entrance of a building where you have an interview in five minutes. You are sitting in your car hoping the heavy rain currently falling will stop soon because you do not have an umbrella. Unfortunately, the rain does not appear to be slowing down. You worry it would make a bad impression if you arrive wet for your interview. You want to be comfortable and appear confident. You assume the offices are air-conditioned and that being wet would make you feel extra cold. You have nothing with you other than a sweater and a very small zippered notebook. Your solution is to hold your sweater above your head and run to the building.

Exaggerated version:

You yank your sunroof out of its frame from the inside of the car and exit your vehicle holding the sunroof over your head. Sure, your car will get soaked through the opening you've just created, but you *really* need this job.

What is problematic about this solution?

The most obvious consequence of this solution is the damage you will do to the sunroof itself. It's going to cost a decent amount to get it repaired. You also may appear a bit foolish or desperate if anyone sees you running into the building holding the sunroof over your head. Carrying the sunroof into the interview definitely would not come across well. If you leave it in the lobby, it may not be there when you get back. The car repair bill will then be even more costly.

Opposite version:

Instead of going to meet your interviewer, have your interviewer come to you. Use your cell to call the person you are supposed to meet with and ask them to use *their* umbrella to come and interview you in your car.

What is problematic about this solution?

This solution will also scream *unprofessional*. Asking the person with more power and authority to cater to your needs will undoubtedly come across as rude and presumptuous.

What do these exaggerated and opposite versions help us to notice about the original solution?

The original solution of using your sweater to shield yourself from the rain:

- does use what you have with you to attempt to solve your problem.

- is something you can do without causing damage to your car.
- will not cost you money to use (no future repair bills).
- doesn't enable you to appear professional and prepared when you arrive at your interview.
- will likely cause you to be feel uncomfortably chilled during the interview since your wet sweater will fail to keep you warm in the air-conditioned office.

What other aspects of the original situation might we now want to consider?

- the usability of other parts of the car
- using something to shield yourself from the rain that will not make you feel chilled when you arrive
- using something to shield yourself from the rain that will not make you look completely idiotic if you are seen walking into the lobby with it
- using something to shield yourself from the rain that will not be difficult to store while you are at your interview
- exploring the possibility of someone in the building, other than the interviewer, bringing an umbrella to you

NEW IDEAS these considerations might spark:

- Perhaps call the receptionist and ask if there is anyone who could bring an umbrella out to you. This could be perceived as pushy or resourceful. It could go either way.
- Use something such as the floor mat – preferably from the backseat, as it may be cleaner – to shield yourself from the rain. You could roll it up and carry it into the interview with you – either ignoring it or calling attention to your creativity. You could also leave it in an unobtrusive corner of the reception area until your interview is finished.

Problem Example 2:
Job sharing

Imagine you are a manger who wants two employees to share one job position. Your solution is to have each of the two employees work one half of every day. One would work mornings and the other afternoons.

Exaggerated version

One employee will work the first half of the year and the other one the second half of the year.

What is problematic about this solution?

A big downside to this solution would be how much catching up the second employee would need to do when they take over at the beginning of the second half of the year. They would not be aware of what has happened, why it happened, or what needs to happen next. A secondary issue may be that other people in the company might need time to begin to trust the competency of the second person.

Opposite version

Instead of splitting each day into two work sessions, you schedule both employees to work all day together on Mondays, Tuesdays, and Wednesday mornings. You figure the two employees will be able to get all the work done by working side-by-side for half the week.

What is problematic about this solution?

The most negative impact of this solution is that both of the employees will be unavailable to their coworkers, clients/customers, managers, and others for the second half of the week.

A secondary issue may be the additional space and equipment required for two people to simultaneously inhabit the current work environment.

What do the exaggerated and opposite versions help us to notice about the original solution?

The original solution of splitting each day into a morning and afternoon shift:

- does divide the work equally between two employees.
- does not require any additional workspace or equipment.
- may necessitate scheduled time for the morning person to update the incoming afternoon person each day.
- may require a non-face-to-face method for the afternoon person to update the incoming morning shift person.
- would require a willingness on the part of the other employees to have faith in the competency of each of the employees based on their ability to stay current with what is happening in the company.

What other aspects of the original situation might we now want to consider?

- the need for transition time
- the possibility of dividing *both* job duties and shifts
- the positives and negatives of dividing the work tasks into two separate jobs
- the availability and analysis of all the resources available
- the costs and benefits of applying particular resources to the situation

NEW IDEAS/ACTIONS these considerations might spark:

- Perhaps check with your employees to see if five half-days or two and a half full-days works better for them.

- Create a very clear division of labor, paying special attention to any job tasks that both employees will need to be ready to perform during their shifts.

- Organize a detailed method of electronic and/or manual communication between the two employees delineating what: 1) has been done; 2) needs to be done; and 3) and any pertinent factors affecting resources, actions, and communications.

- Create an efficient and effective method for the two employees to report to a manager without duplication of efforts.

- Brief the other employees and any other relevant parties about the specific job duties and schedules of the two employees.

Notes:

You're done, but are you finished?

Are you satisfied yet? Should you be?

We often get excited when we generate an idea or a solution we think is clever, especially if it resonates with us personally, and we can imagine other people also connecting easily with it. Perhaps we are quite pleased with a logo we've designed. We believe it will grab people's attention, reel them in, and cause them to be more likely to take the time to further investigate the business or organization the logo represents. If we find ourselves immediately pleased with a solution we have crafted, we may automatically assume those who will apply it will be equally delighted with what we have devised. But will they? How confident are we about our confidence? How can we be sure our high level of satisfaction is warranted?

This brings us to the Third *Do* Key Principle:

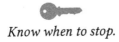

Know when to stop.

One way to spot-check the validity of these self-congratulatory feelings is to imagine you are unable to use your idea. You don't have to create a reason for why you can't use it, just imagine it's suddenly unattainable or unacceptable. Don't do this merely as a gratuitous mental exercise – try to act as if it is truly gone. Imagine how you would actually behave if you were told there was no way you could go forward with your fabulous idea. How long do you think it would take you to shake off your disappointment and begin to attempt to come up with another idea? How would you help yourself to dig deeply, leap bravely, and explore other options? What aspects of your current idea or solution could you use as a starting point to create something different? Still pretending your desired idea isn't possible, choose one of its characteristics as the bones of a possible replacement idea. Perhaps one of your idea's major characteristics could become the primary foundation for another viable idea. Your goal would be to flesh it out differently than you did the first time.

You could then put this first replacement idea aside and dream up a second alternative radically different from your original idea in at least a couple of ways. Sketching it out in broad strokes with a list of suggested steps for developing the idea further would help you to communicate your idea to others. It would also be useful to note any envisioned benefits or potential problems.

What might you learn from these two short journeys? Your original idea may still vibrate with the same allure and potential, or it may now seem slightly less spectacular even though it's still attractive. Perhaps one of your alternative ideas will help you to discover something missing from your original idea or solution, or there may be an aspect from one of these just-generated ideas you can use to embellish or improve your original idea. Compare the components that comprise each of your three ideas. Notice how they differ from each other. Then identify the primary element of each idea, the one that functions as the backbone upon which the idea is built. Note which components are non-negotiable and necessary to make each idea work. Ask yourself what *could* be altered without changing the effectiveness of the core idea. Determine if any of the components are codependent and unable to perform their function without the presence of another component. Does this dependence strengthen or weaken the idea? Imagine how alterations would affect the tone or flavor of each idea. Reassess your judgment of your original idea after you've gone through this exploration process. What do you think now?

Real life example:

Imagine you are about to bake cookies for guests who will arrive in a little over an hour. Your guests include two longtime friends and their three young sons. You envision offering them yummy chocolate chip cookies. You begin to place the ingredients you will need to make the cookies on the counter. You discover you are out of eggs. It is difficult to make really good chocolate chip cookies without them. You live 30 minutes from town; there is not enough time to get the ingredients from the store and make the cookies before your guests arrive. You could go to the store, buy some eggs, get home in time to meet your guests, and then make the cookies with the boys. But you aren't sure they would enjoy baking cookies and you really want to have a snack ready for them. You have your heart set on making cookies, but most cookie recipes include eggs. You decide there are two things you really like about your original chocolate chip choice: 1) many children usually like this type of cookie; and 2) the cookies have chocolate in them. You think of another kind of cookie most children like, one that also has chocolate in it, no-bake chocolate oatmeal cookies. Eggs are not required to make them. If you hadn't analyzed what it was you liked about your first choice you might not have thought of making no-bake cookies.

Your guests are arriving on a beautiful summer day. You envision the three boys enjoying a game of croquet on your lawn with an old set you have in the garage. When they arrive you show them the game. They have no desire to play. They think the game is silly, especially the wickets. It also appears they don't have the patience to follow the rules. They do seem to be full of energy and ready to be active. You decide to use the mallets and the balls to set up a competition to see who can whack their ball the farthest. Everyone chooses a ball and lines up across the yard and attempts to hit their ball farther than everyone else. The boys love it. One of them gets the idea to do the same thing but to try to make the ball end up as close to the base of the oak tree at the far end of the yard without going past it. This game is also a hit. You all continue to create variations of these *whacking* games. Once again you have analyzed the components of an existing idea, this time the game of croquet, and used some of those components in a different fashion to create a new idea. You kept the backbone of your original idea – whacking balls around the yard – but altered it to fit the needs of your particular audience. You achieved your original intention – to engage the boys in a yard game they would enjoy. The boys continued your practice of altering the game's components to create multiple versions of the original game. All of the versions were designed around whacking the balls, and each produced a yard game enjoyable to these young boys.

Being able to discern which component is the backbone of an idea can be quite helpful. Identifying the various individual components of an idea and how they work together to create the idea's essence is also valuable. Sometimes, however, we can become overly enchanted by one of our idea's components. It seems to grab and monopolize our focus.

Don't be blinded by one or two amazing characteristics.

Real life example:

Imagine you are considering dating a particular person. Your friend advises you not to date them: *Don't go out with him. I know he's gorgeous but I hear he's a real SOB. He cheats on everyone he dates. This is not just a rumor, I've heard about him from at least four people he's been with. They all say the same thing.* Or maybe they tell you: *Oh yeah, she's hot, too hot to handle. She's gone ballistic and wrecked quite a few of her dates' lives. If you want her calling your boss and following you around, by all means go out with her.* These sound like helpful warnings, but maybe this gorgeous or hot human is totally into you and there is something about them that really excites you, something that makes you willing to overlook all the sincere, not to mention accurate, warnings you've been given. Really? You sure you want to go there?

It's easy to get distracted by what appeals to us. You may feel overly drawn toward one of the showy or unusual components of an idea you are assessing. Sound familiar? While it is good to identify the qualities that appeal to us – whether we are talking about food, books, movies, potential lovers, or ideas – don't be seduced into hyper-focusing on these stand-out shiny aspects or you may end up not noticing other less attractive, or perhaps even harmful, traits. Creative ideas can be a lot like seductive humans. Shiny-induced myopia might also cause you to miss another aspect of your idea that needs only the barest tweak or polishing to be just as spectacular as the one currently hogging all your attention. Why is this important? Another aspect of your idea may shift your creation's design by becoming the new backbone or driver, or it may, once developed just a bit more, work in tandem with your originally discovered shiny aspect to create an even stronger or more effective solution.

One small factor could end up tanking your creation.

Everything about your idea or solution needs to contribute to fulfilling the purpose or *why* behind your impetus for creating it. No one part should cause a negative impact on either the final application or on another of the creation's components. Be merciless. If something is causing harm, get rid of it. No matter how invested you are in that particular component. If it doesn't help create the desired effect, cut it. You may need to retrofit a replacement for a harmful component if its function is vital to the success of your overall design in some way. It's seductive to plow ahead without taking the needed time to make sure each component of your creation is optimal or, at the very least, that none of them are subpar or harmful. Later, after time and money have been invested, it may be too late to make sorely needed changes. One of the most famous examples of a single component tanking an enterprise concerns the Chevy Nova®. When Chevrolet decided to market the car in Mexico, they forgot to consider what *Nova* means in Spanish. In English it represents a star of unusual brightness. In Spanish *no va* translates to *no go*. Not exactly what one hopes for from their vehicle. The debacle of attempting to market the *Nova* in Mexico represents an allegiance to a particular model that rendered the manufacturers less capable of discerning how the product's name actually made the vehicle undesirable in this new environment. It can happen to the best of us and often does. Being cognizant of this human tendency ahead of time and forcing ourselves to carefully analyze each component of our creative product or plan for its effect on the final outcome can help us to forestall the disastrous consequences of shiny-induced myopia.

Satisfy all the deliverables.

Not only does each component of your idea or solution need to do its part well, the combination of your idea's parts and their interplay must satisfy all the needs of your creative task. Don't stop developing until they do. Revisit your original goals. Do you understand them clearly? Have they changed? Do you need to define any of them more specifically? Analyze your creation. Note how it does or does not satisfy each of the needs you've identified as needing to be met. Once again be merciless. Don't rush. A problem you ignore now may reveal itself later and cause mischief that is much more difficult to handle. This can become a huge problem if it happens after commitments have been made and certain resources are no longer available for making a large change you could have made easily in an earlier stage of the process.

Let's look at two taglines and analyze how they each satisfy all the important needs they were commissioned to address.

- Ajax® *Stronger than dirt*
- Alka-Seltzer® *I can't believe I ate the whole thing*

The first one, for Ajax® cleanser, is a straightforward and in-your-face kind of tagline. The second one, for Alka-Seltzer®, is a bit more implied. Let's examine them a little further. Ajax® certainly wanted to convey how strong and powerful their product is. They could have come up with alternative taglines such as: *Stronger than strong* or *Out cleans other cleaners.*

The first alternative gets across how strong the product is but it leaves us wondering: strong in *what* way? The second alternative lets us know it's better than other cleaners but we are still unaware of what it can *do*. Their actual tagline does it all. *Stronger than dirt* emphasizes how *strong* the product is and also makes us aware of what that strength can do, namely overpower *dirt*. This helps us to realize the product not only will help us clean but will also conquer any and all dirtiness it encounters. This is what we care about – getting rid of dirt. And, if it's *stronger* than the dirt then the dirt doesn't have a chance, and we assume that means cleaning will be easy for us when we are armed with Ajax®. That's an enormous amount of meaning from three little words. Each word is a component of this tagline's message. Each represents a concept the company wants us to understand about their product. Nothing is wasted. Everything contributes. Each word is a good word. *Stronger* tells us it's powerful, and the words *than dirt* work together to let us know the level of strength and what that strength can accomplish. Perfection. *Stronger than filth* would not have worked because *filth* has other connotations and we don't want to think of our homes as filthy. Dirty is fine but filthy goes too far. *Tougher than dirt* wouldn't work nearly as well because it doesn't imply it can overpower dirt the way *stronger* does. Together these three words communicate the powerfulness and quality of the product and how well it will clean for the user. Everything is satisfied.

The Alka-Seltzer® tagline, *I can't believe I ate the whole thing*, has more of an implied message. This tagline was originally presented in numerous commercials that each showed someone noticeably uncomfortable from overeating who dramatically delivered the tagline with great disbelief and regret. Each speaker seemed appalled that their own poor judgment had led them to their current physical distress. The obvious in-our-face disbelief expressed by each of these poor schlubs who had overeaten, even though they should have known they would be miserable afterwards, demonstrated a type of bad choice familiar to many of us. This familiarity implied that this type of overeating happens regularly. And the makers of Alka-Seltzer® were telling us that Alka-Seltzer® would be there to rescue us every time. If you decide to craft a subtle message, make sure the solution it represents not only satisfies all of your creative project's criteria but that it will be clearly understood by your audience. If your intended audience doesn't *get* your message or your solution, it will not work. It doesn't matter whether your audience is your child, your parent, your lover, your manager, or a specific segment of the general public, if a seemingly perfect message or solution is not clearly understood it cannot do what it was designed to do. Don't let attempts to craft a more sophisticated message (or solution) end up reducing your audience's comprehension of your creation. Sometimes it can be useful to start with the most ridiculous, obvious, and in-your-face idea and then slowly finesse it to make it more understated and elegant. Be sure your audience will be able to *get* the message when you have crafted your final subtle creation. If they don't, tweak it in a manner that dials your message or solution back toward the obvious. You can be as subtle as you would like as long as you do not sacrifice your audience's understanding to get there. Why might you want to be subtle? Because sometimes being subtle can be smoother, sexier, or more entertaining.

Imagine you are with a group of people tasked to create a PR event to promote awareness of the lack of access to clean water experienced by people in many parts of the world. Someone in the group asks what would help people to *feel* the reality of the situation. Someone else shouts out, *Let's make them really, really thirsty.* Someone then suggests you host a long hot event, perhaps over an entire day, in which the attendees are corralled in the hot sun and denied any access to water. This is obviously an outrageous and potentially harmful idea. But what if this ridiculous idea could be morphed into a fabulous idea by tweaking it into a subtler but equally can't-miss-the-message idea? Your thought process could go from making your guests experience thirst to demonstrating how fortunate *they* are to have access to a cup of clean water to drink and how much less fortunate *others* are. This type of thinking could generate the idea to serve clear fresh water in compostable cups with a fill line drawn showing: 1) the number of ounces of water contained in the cup; 2) the distance people living in a specific location in the world would have to walk to acquire their water; and 3) the percentage of their daily allotment of water the amount in the cup represents for those same people. This subtler message would be highly effective at getting your intended point across to your audience. This idea generation process requires everyone to have permission to throw out ridiculous, partially formed ideas without fearing judgment from others. Remember to give yourself this same permission when you are working on your own. Don't judge your initial ideas. Tweak and morph them to perfection.

Get yourself from clever to excellent.

Many of us equate being creative with the ability to brainstorm and generate new ideas. Being truly creative, however, means being able to develop those ideas into excellent versions that satisfy all the needs of your creative task and easily reach your intended audience. This requires you, as a creator, to assess how your initial ideas connect to both the task's requirements and to your anticipated audience's comprehension. Don't stop developing too soon. Don't settle for something that is merely clever. That's right, clever is your starting place not your endpoint. When you come up with something clever it will tickle your fancy and excite you. That's good. Now, figure out why you feel an affinity with this seedling of an idea. Whatever it is that makes it shine is the part you need to develop so that it does more than merely grab your attention. Remember to be willing to consider that you aren't finished yet even if you are immediately pleased with what has just come out of your mouth. Take a moment. Analyze it. What's good about it? What's missing? What needs to be cut? Seedlings are very exciting when they sprout up. Where there was nothing, suddenly there is something and it appears to be fresh and lovely. But it may not yet be mature enough to satisfy your task's needs.

Enjoy your seedling's arrival, and then figure out how to develop it. My students often presented passionate cases for using their seedlings as their final creative products. They would tell me over and over how wonderful their seedlings were. I would tell them that if they had to convince me their seedlings were wonderful then they most likely were not. I then would show them how these early creations might be misunderstood, misleading, incomplete, the wrong tone, cliché, or too predictable. Still they would argue to keep them. Finally when faced with the potential of a 'D' grade they would finally begin to develop their seedling ideas. They always came up with something substantially better. They would fall in love with their new ideas. They would look back at their seedlings and wonder why they had ever been so enamored and argued so fiercely to keep them. Eventually they came to recognize seedlings for what they are – good places to start. They began, when looking at early ideas, to utter statements such as: *Well it's good but I think we can do better* and *It's catchy but it doesn't quite get our purpose across.*

I went through this seedling-ideas-to-better-ideas journey when I needed to create a name for a deck of cards I designed to help people reflect on what's currently going on in their lives. The deck consists of 51 cards. Each of the cards has a common object – a *thing* pictured on it. These include things such as candles, towers, shoes, and buildings. Each of these things belongs to a group of three; there are three types of lights, three types of trucks, three types of hats, and so on for each category of items pictured in the deck. The deck employs a 3-card spread that helps the user to explore and reflect on what these items may represent to them about their lives. At first I was going to call the deck: *Thingamajigs* and have a tagline that read *reflections on the dance of life*. The obvious connections are:

- The *thing* portion of *Thingamajigs* represents the fact that there are *things* pictured on all of the cards.
- The *jig* portion of *Thingamajigs* represents the *dance of life* mentioned in the tagline.

Although this is a whimsical and fun name that does relate somewhat to the product I had created, it didn't clearly communicate the purpose of the deck to my audience. It did correspond to the *thing* nature of the deck but not to the usage of the deck. The tagline was actually created after the fact to make the name *mean more* than it did all on its own. Sometimes this can work well; sometimes it feels a little or a lot forced. This felt like one of those forced times. I could have tweaked it and called it *Thing-a-me-jigs* to get across that the deck has something to do with the *me* who would be using it and with a dance, *the jig*, but that felt even more forced and more confusing. I knew it wasn't right. It had the wrong tone; it was far too silly to match the reflective purpose of the cards. The deck was designed to be used similarly to a tarot deck. Someone else could use the deck to *read* your cards for you, but if you used them on your own, the goal was to reflect on what each of the three cards in the spread were asking you to consider. There would be an accompanying manual to guide you in this exploration. Many people enjoy tarot cards and find them enjoyable to use but it's not a whimsical pastime. It's a somewhat serious pursuit that often ends up being an entertaining experience as well.

My gut told me the name was wrong. Some people liked it. They thought it was *cute*. As soon as they used that word I was sure the name needed to be something different. But what was it about the original name that I liked? The *thing* aspect was a really big deal for me. I wanted to focus on the fact that this deck featured *things* from our daily lives. I even liked having the word *thing* in the name and hoped to keep it. The *jig* portion was more of a conceptual component of the name. I liked what it represented: *the dance of life and thus reflections upon that dance,* yet it was apparent that the name alone did not convey this concept clearly. The goal then became to capture the reflective nature of the deck. I was stuck and needed to step away from attempting to evolve the name. I gave the name a wide berth for a while. Whenever it would pop into my head I'd consider it for a few moments but no more. I let the back of my brain, my subconscious, play with it as much as it wanted but I strongly believed that trying to actively force it would get me nowhere, or worse, somewhere horrible. I had learned from prior experiences that rushing to come up with something to replace the wrong name would probably result in another equally wrong name. Urgency was not my friend so I stayed chill. I trusted the name would come. I could do this because I knew I had given my subconscious what it needed to work on the name without me. It was aware of what was *right* about the wrong name and what was *undesirable* about it.

The final name popped into my head after some time had gone by, time in which much simmering was taking place in the back of my head. My subconscious was noticing everything I encoun-tered and scanning it for possible resources for a new name. It hit pay dirt a few weeks later. I was having cake and coffee with two friends at the front bar in one of our favorite restaurants. I was using the cards and reading them for my friends. One of the co-owners came up to the bar and asked me to read her cards. I did. There was a woman sitting next to one of my friends at the bar. It turned out she was visiting from out of state, and was in town to see a band playing on the waterfront later that night. She kept eying the cards. I asked her if she had a question. She did, but first she asked me to explain the cards to her. I said they were more or less like tarot cards and if used without a reader could help the user to reflect on a specific aspect of their life. *Oh, kind of like the I Ching,* she said. I agreed that this was so and then I read her cards for her several times. We all had a blast. A couple of days later I was revisiting ideas for the deck. I still wanted the word *thing* as part of the name to represent the items pictured on the cards. I also wanted the name to stand alone and convey the purpose of the cards without a tagline. Suddenly, the woman from the bar's comment about the deck being similar to the *I Ching* rose up to my consciousness, and ZAP, *ThingChing* was born. It felt like a much better name than *Thingamajigs.* Glad I didn't stick with my first *clever* idea; glad I was willing to let the idea simmer long enough to evolve into a name that would mean more to my audience. Or so I thought. When I tried the name out with various people, many of them either hadn't heard of the *I Ching* or they simply didn't *get* the name *ThingChing.* The name didn't work for my audience. I had to rethink. I went back to the purpose of the cards: to ask questions in order to obtain guidance through reflection. *Wise Asks* became the name. It captures these two major concepts well. *Asks* speaks to the questions asked by the deck users. *Wise* speaks to the wisdom these seekers will hopefully gain. The fact that the name comically sounds a bit like *wise ass* is a bonus and a nod to not taking the whole thing too seriously.

Don't stop developing too soon. Take the time to honestly analyze your ideas. Don't do the equivalent of hitting a good tennis serve and admiring it so much that the ball comes whizzing back over the net to hit you in the head. Being pleased with your cleverness is fine; just don't get so fixated on it that you settle for something that isn't fully formed, that doesn't satisfy all your requirements, or won't clearly convey your message to your audience.

Finally, consider the impact of what you have created. First look at how your idea sits within the system for which it has been designed. How does it affect what is right around it? In order to determine this, you must be aware of everything within its immediate contact area. This includes other things, people, and places. Then look outside that immediate area. Are there any other potential points of impact you need to consider as you analyze the initial impact of your creative idea or solution? Will any of these impacts cause ripple or domino effects? A truly excellent creation is designed for its immediate purpose and location, and also takes into account what else will affect it and what it might affect in turn. Make sure your creation adds value in its primary placement and adds value or, at the very least, does no harm in any adjacent or chain reaction areas both physical and philosophical. Truly excellent creations add value and do no harm. Make sure this is true of your creation, whatever it is.

EXERCISES
to help you not stop too soon

Exercise 1:
A really good one

Come up with an idea you think is a good one for a particular creative project. It can be something simple such as a party theme or a particularly mischievous practical joke. Write a short description of your idea. Include a few overview details to convey the essence of the idea but don't worry about including specifics at this point.

Now, set that idea aside and come up with two more good ideas for the same endeavor. Review all three ideas. Identify which of the three you like the most at this point, without giving any extra positive weight to your original idea as you decide. Make note of your choice. Now, flesh out and add specific details to each idea in an attempt to make them all equally amazing. Pretend each idea, as you work on it, is the one you will ultimately use. Don't play favorites; give all three your full focus. Ask yourself how you can make each one the best it can be. Develop each idea fully. Make them all spectacular.

Now which idea is your favorite? Is it your original idea or one of the ones you added? What makes it your favorite? Most of us have a tendency to immediately prefer one idea over another idea. We like its cleverness or we are particularly drawn to one of its characteristics. This not only invites us to avoid developing it, it also can pull our focus away from other ideas that may be even better. Practice letting go of your first idea. Set it aside knowing you can get back to it later. Generate a second idea. Develop this idea more fully. Go back and develop your first idea more fully too. This is a good way to teach yourself to turn clever ideas into excellent ideas by developing them a little bit further.

Exercise 2:
The perfect gift

Think of two or three good friends or family members. Write down their names. Under each name list three characteristics you feel accurately describe that person. For each person, write a gift idea next to each of their listed characteristics that *fits* that particular aspect of their personality. An example would be a DVD of a hilarious British comedy for a friend with a dry sense of humor or a French New Wave movie for someone with artsy taste.

Your first three gift ideas were probably pretty good, maybe even fabulous, but try now to think of a gift that would fit all three characteristics. It may be more difficult to come up with this composite gift idea. Did the first three ideas help or hinder your attempts to generate an all-in-one gift idea? How can you use what you've learned in this exercise to be more successful at generating ideas and solutions that satisfy all the aspects of your next creative project?

Exercise 3:
Dream big, then scale it back

Describe in amazing detail what your fantasy vacation would involve if money, time, and availability didn't matter. Now imagine you have to dial it back. Perhaps you want to go to the ocean, but it's so far from your home that going there would require an amount of time and money you cannot afford to invest at the moment. How could you scale back your dream yet still *get* the essence of what you want?

Start by identifying the characteristics that most appeal to you. Is it the water itself that calls to you? Do you hope to spend hours being in the water? Or, does the ocean represent natural wonder and majesty? Perhaps it's all about sunbathing or walking uninterrupted in the beauty of nature. For some people the joy of being at the ocean is hearing the rhythm of the powerful waves. Once you identify the components of your dream vacation that are most important to you, you can design an excursion that provides similar effects in a more easily attainable manner. Be inventive. Attempt to replicate the specific feeling you would get from each key aspect of your dream vacation. If your desire is to spend time *in* the water, a lake may be just as satisfying. If what you want is to be *on* the water, a river may make you happy. You may find a well-marked and gentle hiking trail with a gorgeous vista delightful if walking in nature is how you most want to spend your time. A mountain range or other outdoor wonder may serve you well if you're hoping to be awed by nature. If you're looking for a peaceful experience, hot springs may be just what you need. There's really nothing that can replicate the sound of ocean waves; however, the slap-splash of a riverboat paddlewheel or a small waterfall may be enough of a delight to your ears. Your unobtainable dream vacation is just like an amazing idea or solution that doesn't happen to match the project's available resources. Identify the key conceptual characteristics of the fabulous-but-unusable idea or solution you've designed and combine new versions of these vital characteristics – versions that do not require additional resources – into a new and pleasing whole that also elegantly satisfies the requirements of the creative task at hand.

Notes:

Do you rush to procrastinate?

One of the most important things you can do to improve your creative process is to become aware of it. Turn the focus of your observation onto yourself. Notice what you are thinking when you are being creative. Notice what you choose to do. Notice what you decide not to do. Notice what helps your process and what hinders it. Notice what's happening when your creativity suddenly seems to flow easily in a magical and unexpected way. Also notice what causes it to come to an unexpected, screeching, and hopeless halt; and what makes it begin to spew a steady stream of mundane ideas. This brings us to the Third *See* Key Principle:

Become aware of your own process.

Many of us believe that our creative process just *happens*. We don't think we have any control of our creativity. Most of us are usually aware of at least some of the choices we make, but all of our choices have an impact on the formation of our creative process. The trick is to become aware of more of our choices; in fact, the goal is to become aware of as many of our choices as possible. Won't this interrupt our creative flow? Not if we choose our reflection moments wisely.

What motivates you? What deters you?

Start by determining what *helps* you to be creative. This is not the same for everyone. You might need absolute quiet to work, or you might find your process flows much more freely when you're listening to music. What helps one person's creative process drives another person to distraction. Literally. Your ideal circumstances can make others unable to concentrate. In fact, there is undoubtedly someone who would consider your optimal working conditions to be a creative wasteland lacking inspiration or comfort.

You probably already recognize some of what feeds your process, especially obvious things such as whether you need sound or silence, or prefer your surroundings to be messy or neat. But there are many other things that hinder and support your process. In order to figure out what works best for you, you must first notice as many of your behaviors during your creative process as possible. Pay no attention to whether they seem helpful or not. Simply make note of them. This is both easier and harder than it sounds. It's harder because you need to record what you notice either while it's happening or shortly afterwards. Each of these approaches has its advantages. Documenting your behaviors as they are happening helps you to more accurately capture what you're doing; however, taking the time to capture it can change what you would have done in the first place. Some people can keep zinging along their creative flow while simultaneously jotting down notes about what they are doing. Others find that recording *burps* their creative flow and throws them completely off track. Waiting until you're done with a particular stage of your process to record what happened can result in sketchy or inaccurate recollections. A combination of the two done over the course of several projects often produces the best results.

As you begin to compile notes about each step of your creative journey, remember the following:

- You're trying to capture as much as you can, but your primary goal is to stay focused on whatever you are currently working to accomplish.
- The more specific you can be when recording your own behaviors, the more useful the information will be to you.
- Don't judge what you notice. Don't label it as good or bad; simply capture it accurately.
- Notice if your behaviors change based on where you are, at that moment, in your creative process. (Do you need different conditions to brainstorm, for example, than you do to edit and polish?)

Consider the following five types of information as you observe and record your behaviors:

1) Starting points/influencers

These are the seeds or origins of your ideas, the mini-trampolines that catapulted you toward a particular thought:

- Where did they come from?
- What made you think of them?

- Why did you decide to seriously consider them?
- What made you ultimately choose rather than reject them?

2) Leaping points/landing points/re-leaping points/final or near final points

These are the landing points along your string of ideas, the places you progressed to from a previous idea:

- Why did you leap from the first one to the next one?
- What was the connection between the two?
- How long did you stay there before you chose to leap to yet another idea?
- What influenced your successive leaps?
- What made you decide you were done leaping?

3) Choice points

These are all the places where you decided to choose *this* instead of *that*, where you intentionally turned away from one direction to go a different way:

- Why did you leap in one particular direction instead of another?
- What were the internal and external influences that affected your choices?
- Did you consciously make a decision to not leap in a particular direction?
- Did you choose something because it was noticeably *better* than something else in a specific way, or because it just *felt* more interesting?

4) The ways you communicate

These are all the ways you give information to and receive information from yourself and others:

- Did you talk aloud or only in your head?
- When did you share ideas with others, at the beginning or only after your thoughts were more fully formed?
- Did you listen to everyone else's ideas before you spoke, or did you rush to be one of the first to speak?
- Were you irritated or energized by the communications of others?
- Did you need or want others to voice approval for your ideas, or were you happy to appreciate your ideas yourself?
- Was it easy or difficult for you to describe what was going on in your mind to others?

5) Finishing

These are the things you do as a project is coming to a close, the choices you make that determine how the final version will look:

- What convinced you that the project or creative session was finished?
- Did others agree with you when you judged a project as being either finished or not quite done?
- Did you stop because you were truly satisfied or were you just too frustrated to continue?
- Are you the one who always wants to polish just a bit more or the person who cautions against over-tinkering?

Examine the list of observations you've made about your creative process behaviors.

What do you recognize? What did you already realize you do? What surprised you? What were you completely unaware of prior to recording your self-observations? What other types of discoveries did you make? Are there any behaviors you previously thought you did all the time only to discover you barely did them at all? Are there other behaviors you thought you hardly ever did that showed up again and again in your observations? Which of all these types of behaviors do you want to repeat? Are there any you want to scale back on or to rid yourself of altogether?

Select the behaviors that seem to work for you on a consistent basis and repeat them intentionally next time you begin to create. Don't choose too many things to focus on at once. Either choose several overall behaviors or one for each stage of your process. Also notice what seems to be holding you back. Try something else instead. If you can't think of anything, simply plan to not do the unhelpful behavior and see if something rises up to take its place.

Here are some things to be on the lookout for as you hone your awareness of what feeds your creative process. Notice anything and everything that distracts you. Figure out if the distractions you encountered resulted in productive creation, a slowing down of your flow, or the need to reboot back to where you were before the distraction. Many different types of things can *burp* our attention and creative flow. Notice what does that for you. Also notice if you give in to tantrums of frustration that can leave you just as stressed out as you were before you started throwing a fit. Avoid these by recognizing them as the frustration eruptions they are. Figure out how to release some of your frustration in an entertaining, or at the very least, mostly harmless way, or learn to channel that frustration into creative energy. Doing either is good. Doing neither is a soul-sucking choice you will regret. These tantrums also scare off other potentially cool, creative collaborators.

Lose-lose all around. Don't go there.

While there are many aspects of our creative process we have no control over, there are many other choices we do get to make. Some things freak us out when they drone-fly into our creative space without warning. Once they arrive however, we get to decide how to respond to them. We get to choose what to say to others and to ourselves inside our own heads. Be intentional and constructive about your freaking-out response plan.

Also notice wind-up-toy-in-the-corner moments when you seem stuck and unable to continue forward. We've all been to that place where we keep circling back to the same ideas or trying to convince ourselves that something that isn't working actually *is* the solution we have been looking for all along. Observe when these kinds of things happen to you. Notice the conditions when it happens. What were you thinking? Doing? Saying? During what stage of the creation process did it occur? Were you feeling confident or stressed just before it happened? Were you sharing your ideas with others or stuck in your own head? Next time you get into this rut, purposely change a few of those elements. Notice if this intentional tweakage makes a difference. Remember, or better yet record, what happens. Use this new knowledge to continue tweaking toward better future outcomes.

What floats your boat when there isn't any water?

Lots of time + lots of money + lots of interest + lots of confidence + lots of emotional support + comfortable conditions = heaven.

This kind of idyll, the ultimate heavenly set of creative circumstances, rarely happens in most of our creative lives. In fact, often we are expected to or need to, perform in less than ideal conditions. Ask yourself what you would need in order to survive in the worst conditions. Then ask yourself a much more important question: What would you need to thrive in the worst conditions? These are your non-negotiables. These are the *green M&Ms* your creative genius demands to have before each performance. Your creative genius is picky and insistent. It wants you to understand what it needs. It will tell you if you ask. So ask. Figure out what your fussy but talented inner genius needs to perform at the top of its game in various circumstances. Then make sure it gets what it needs.

Sometimes though, your genius will lie to you about what it needs. It doesn't do this on purpose. It gets confused. It truly believes it needs certain things, but sometimes those needs are actually manifestations of fear. Attempting to placate these fears usually won't make them go away. In fact, it often shifts your focus away from your creative process and onto a fruitless and frantic search for unrealized security. This is not a good thing. Tell your inner genius to chill. Convince it that it's okay to make mistakes. Promise you won't get upset if it screws up. Make sure you mean it.

We do some interesting things when we attempt to satisfy the needs of our inner creative genius. Most creative people need or at least crave a rush of excitement in order to jumpstart their process. Some need it to get motivated enough to even begin to intentionally focus their energies on a project. This excitement can come from a passionate interest in the project's topic or purpose, the opportunity to collaborate with amazingly creative colleagues, or from some end reward such as recognition or a large monetary sum. But for some of us, it's not about money or fame. Sure, we want those things at the end of our process, but they don't provide enough juice to get us started. We crave the rush of passionate interest. We need the rush. We feel uninterested and unable to start without it.

Many of us procrastinate and wait until the last possible moment to begin the project as an antidote to passionless situations. The adrenaline rush we experience as we fearfully freak out about not having enough time to meet our deadline provides the juice we need to focus our energies and engage our inner genius. Of course, timing becomes exquisitely critical. If too many things outside of our control go wrong, we won't make the deadline. We might lose a client or the opportunity to prove our worth to a gatekeeper of future opportunities. But sometimes it all comes together. Sometimes, our eleventh-hour rush successfully stokes our inner genius and we end up shining brightly. Those with youth and vitality have the advantage of being able to work at peak performance with little or no sleep, thus being able to do more in the short amount of time they've allotted to their project. But creators of any age who become aware of their creative process can perfect the timing of this practice by noticing what most often makes it successful for them.

Help, I'm stuck up here on this plateau and I don't see any way off!

The beginning of your creative process isn't the only possible sticking point. There are many others. Some of us get to a certain point and then we just can't seem to continue. Perhaps we had more than enough juice at the start of a project to jump in with intense enthusiasm and high levels of engagement, but somewhere along the way we simply lost interest. We're still interested in getting the project finished; we're simply not interested in working on it. The love affair is over. Why does this happen? What can we do when it does?

Some of us find ourselves stuck on a creative plateau because our excitement centers on initiating ideas. We adore the thrill of tackling something new. Once there's a trajectory and the beginning of a plan we find ourselves getting bored. We crave the next challenge. We've tamed this one. It no longer amuses us. This isn't because we are egocentric and spoiled; it's a function of the needs of our particular creative process, our inner creative genius's need for a steady diet of energy. Some of us get that energy from conceiving new ideas. Others get it from developing ideas. Still others get it from perfecting and polishing ideas. The lucky among us get energy from two or more stages of the creative process.

If you're part of a creative team, you can take turns leading the parts of the process that energize you. If you're on your own or partnered with someone who either has your same energy requirements or needs you to work with them to get things done, you're screwed unless you discipline yourself to slog through the parts that bore you. Slogging doesn't produce brilliant results but it can force your inner genius to be engaged. It will drag its feet. It will complain. It will moan and whine and swear it has nothing to offer. Do not believe it. If you don't give up, if you stick with it, your inner genius will eventually, albeit reluctantly, begin to function. Reward it. Find a way to give it what it needs. If initiating ideas is what feeds it, focus on that aspect of the development stage. Explore adding something new or doing something a new way to tweak and improve your project. Frame each iteration as a new beginning. Find out what makes the development stage less painful for your initiation-stage-hungry inner genius. It takes discipline to stick with something when you're not interested. This is true for everyone but especially true for creatives. This does not give you permission to be undisciplined. Most successful creatives have a practice that effectively melds passion and discipline. Noticing and becoming aware of your process can help you to discover the actions and habits that will help you successfully calibrate the balance between these two necessary ingredients in various creative circumstances.

There is another reason creators get stuck alone on a desolate plateau – fear. We believe in what we're doing. We think the project is developing beautifully. But suddenly we lose confidence that others will see it the way we do. Some part of us believes that if we never complete our project it will never have the chance to fail. This is both true and not true. While it's true that we won't create a failure if we don't finish our project, we will also keep ourselves from finishing, which is in itself a type of failing. Sometimes it takes more courage to finish a project than it does to choose to attempt it in the first place. Discipline can get you through, but here's the thing – if you're not ready to finalize your project, you're not going to be truly motivated and engaged. You can't force yourself to function as your best creative self when you're mired in fear. No one else can either. They can force you to work but not to excel. But you'll never lose the fear if you don't give continuing forward a shot, one small creative choice, one small creative step at a time. Learn what helps you to silence or muffle the fear. Learn what you need to say to yourself and what you need others to say to you. Learn what you have to remind yourself of and what you have to forget about, at least for the moment. Your inner genius is your instrument. Learn how to keep it from becoming immobilized by fear. Learn how to get the most out of it under a variety of circumstances.

EXERCISES
to help you figure out what works for you

The Exercise:
Notice and record what you observe about your creative process

Version 1:
Sense what works

Experiment by changing your working conditions and discovering how different choices affect your ability to create.

Start with sound. Play music while you work. Listen to different types of music: music with and without words; music you know and music you don't know; and different genres of music that are softer or quieter, faster or slower. Also try background noises such as fans or other types of white noise. Notice what gives you energy and helps you focus, and what distracts you.

Do the same thing with your surroundings. Try working in a place with a lot of visual stimulation; then try somewhere more stark, with fewer visuals or less motion.

Also notice what kinds of clothes make your feel comfortable enough or serious enough to create. You might need total comfort or you might benefit from clothing that sends a *this is important* message to you. Notice what works for you.

Version 2:
Positions everyone!

Try brainstorming sitting down, standing up, and walking. Notice when you want to move and when you want to sit still. Try to do what your body and mind ask you to do. If you aren't getting any messages from your body, simply try different methods and notice how each one affects your creative process.

Version 3:
Comfort and rituals

Figure out what makes you feel comfortable and secure. Do you need a special pen? Do you like to use a certain kind of paper or a particular font size on your computer screen? What makes you feel in control of your own process? These small things can seem ridiculously unimportant, but if they matter to you, they *are* important. They can help to ground you, to make you feel as if it's safe or easy to begin your creative process.

Version 4:
Find out how you roll

What helps you process ideas? Some creatives need to type what they are thinking and then read it out loud to make their ideas make sense, to themselves and to others. They may also be seen constantly making notes in a journal they carry everywhere. When these creatives are part of a creative team, they may also type or write what everyone else says to help themselves process the various ideas presented.

Other people simply need to talk out loud in order to process their thoughts. They are more than willing to put forth half-formed ideas because they continue to develop them as they speak.

Some people need to create a visual representation or diagram of what they are thinking. You would expect this behavior from artists, but there are some people with only so-so drawing skills who *need* to sketch to think. Are you one of them?

And of course, there are those people who keep everything in their heads. They usually listen, ponder, and then speak.

There's no wrong way to do this. If you already know what works for you, become more aware of how you are doing it, AND do it on purpose more often. If you don't already know how you roll through your creative process, try some of the methods mentioned here and see which one seems to make creative thinking easier for you.

Version 5:
Later!

Try taking a break in the middle of your project. Go take a walk, read a book, or watch a movie. Go back to your project. Notice if you seem to have processed subconsciously during your break, and if the inner work you did helped you to move forward with your project. If this works well for you, plan on scheduling it into your next creative task.

Do looming deadlines spur you on? You might be someone who uses the rush you get from the fear-of-not-making-a-deadline to good advantage. If this describes you, practice waiting long enough to get the rush while still leaving yourself enough time for polishing, and not missing that deadline. Notice what works so you can repeat it next time.

Version 6:
Sharing your ideas

Notice how and when you communicate your ideas to others. Try sharing your ideas with someone else as soon as they pop into your head. Then try developing them on your own before you share them with anyone. Which way works best to help you advance your ideas?

Version 7:
Eeny, meeny, miny moe

Notice the choices you make during your creative process. Identify why you chose one thing over another. What *caused* you to judge one idea as better or worse than another one? Did a thought or experience cause you to see the discarded idea in a less favorable light? Try to capture your process. Pay particular attention to those moments when making choices flows easily, and to those moments when you feel hesitant or stuck. Notice what you were doing, saying, and thinking during each of these types of moments. Plan to intentionally repeat those behaviors and habits that seemed to affect your creative process in positive ways.

Notes:

8

Why should I work with them?

Some of us get excited at the prospect of working on a creative project with others. Some of us just want to be left alone to do our own thing. Sometimes we are required to work with others. Sometimes, we *need* other people because of a prolonged creative block, or because the job is too big for any one person to complete during the time allotted. You may be concerned working with others will get in the way of your own creative success, but we often end up with *more* when we work creatively with others. More minds to pinpoint what's needed to accomplish a particular creative pursuit. More eyes to uncover previously unnoticed resources. More brains filled with memories that will cause additional leaps to new ideas and solutions. More noses for sniffing out potential collateral damage and benefits. Of course you are also likely to get more disagreements, dissimilar processing styles, and conflicting egos. Don't let the potentially annoying components of working with others keep you from benefiting from the many good things others can contribute to your creative process.

Work done by a creative team is a collective pursuit and it usually receives collective appreciation or disapproval. Work done by the collective is often jointly owned by the group or by whoever hired them. Of course you can use a consultant or request assistance from a friend and still *own* your creative outcome. But claiming another's work as your own is never cool. Make sure the terms surrounding your collaborations aren't murky. Be intentionally transparent about any compensation, acknowledgment, or ownership to anyone who helps you with your creative pursuits, whether personal or professional. If you feel uncomfortable describing the terms of a creative collaboration to someone who is helping you, it is quite possible you should also feel uncomfortable about the way you have decided to structure those terms. Reflect on what you want the outcome of your collaboration to be. Do a little research to discover how to ethically design what you envision.

A lack of clarity about a working collective's creative purpose can adversely affect the group's process and outcome. Take the time, whether working with one other person or an entire creative team, to clearly define what you are trying to accomplish together. Do not misstep into attempting to predetermine *how* you will achieve your goals, but rather craft a shared vision of what will be *different* when the group has completed its task. Then work together to figure out innovative ways to manifest that difference.

IOU or you-owe-me

Sometimes, members of a creative collective want to be acknowledged for their individual contributions. For some members, an in-the-moment brightening of their teammates' eyes, or an excitedly voiced, *Yes, yes, that will work well,* is all they desire. Others also crave some type of official recognition when the group's work is completed. Disagreements about how credit should be allocated can potentially hamper the group's creative process. Certain individuals may hesitate to share ideas if they believe they won't receive any credit, while others may be likely to forcefully advance their ideas mistakenly hoping to *earn* more credit than others. Transparent communication among group members goes a long way to help forestall misunderstandings; however, an active acceptance, by all members, of the terms and conditions of working together is necessary to keep the creative process untainted by individual frustrations and resentments. In some creative collectives, individual contributions are acknowledged only within the group; in other collectives, managers or clients are made aware of individual contributions. Each member needs to accept the working conditions set for their current project and not allow them to negatively affect their individual contributions or attitude. Members of the collective who harbor discontent or resentment, for whatever reason, may find themselves unintentionally derailing their own creative process and that of other members, or of the collective as a whole.

Who are these other creative people you could end up working with?

Extremely creative people are often portrayed as highly energetic and extroverted. They are also usually depicted as having little regard for what others think of their choices. Sometimes a creative genius is portrayed as a loner introvert, often with wildly unkempt hair. But there is no one type of creative person. Being an extrovert is not a requirement for being creative. Nor is being odd or unusual. A middle-aged person dressed in a somewhat nondescript outfit, who at first glance appears dim or disconnected from the current conversation, may blow up your preconceived stereotype when they spontaneously begin to offer one intriguing idea after another. Keep in mind others may also have preconceived notions of what a creative person looks and sounds like, and it may or may not resemble you. Don't defend your creativity; demonstrate it in constructive and discernable ways. Don't show off; show up.

What do other creatives actually contribute?

We all bring different attributes to a creative collective. Some rare individuals possess the ability to excel at every part of the creative process. Others are reasonably proficient overall while truly excelling at one or two aspects. Others shine very brightly during one stage of the process and coast through the rest. When we tackle creative tasks on our own, we must fill every creative *role* ourselves. When we work creatively with others, we often benefit from their ability to excel in the roles we feel the least confident shouldering. This is why it's good to play with others.

What roles need to be filled for a successful creative collaboration?

Creative team roles represent different aspects and stages of a group's creative process. Individual members often function in one or more roles. There are various ways of labeling these roles. Here is one way to do it:

Generators

These individuals seem *magically blessed* with the ability to instantly and effortlessly generate one good idea after another. They may appear to pull good ideas out of the ether. Often, we are unable to easily perceive a generator's thought process. Skilled generators can continue to spew fabulous ideas until they present one everyone agrees should be used. Generators usually possess the ability to leap instantly from any of their own ideas to additional ideas that are just as good if not better. They can also generate new ideas or tweak their original ideas based on their teammates' comments. Generators don't embarrass easily. This allows them to use any *bad* ideas they generate as springboards to *good* ideas.

Developers

These *insightful* people seem to instinctively know how to advance an initial idea to the next stage. They are usually extremely talented at perceiving the multiple concepts contained within an initial idea. This helps them to see an abundance of connection possibilities. Developers can switch from one possible connection to another with lightning speed. Nothing seems to deter their determined march toward weaving aspects of an initial idea into a more comprehensive creation that perfectly satisfies the group's creative goals in obvious yet inventive ways.

Researchers

These *Indiana Joneses* of the creative process seem to be able to find just about anything: information, images, outdated sources, practical resources, expert advice, *whatever* the group's process may currently require. They usually are also skilled at recognizing and subsequently teasing out component parts from a *whole* and then using them to elegantly satisfy a particular creative need.

Orchestrators

These creative *conductors* seem to be aware of all the moving components within a creative process. They also sense how these parts should be combined to create the group's intended goal. They often see what needs to happen before those who are in the momentary thick of the actual process do. A truly skilled orchestrator enlists and excites their group mates rather than conducting in an impatient and know-it-all fashion.

Polishers

These detail-oriented people seem to have an innate ability to *retain and juggle* the many discrete requirements of a creative task. Polishers know how to make things shiny and alluring while satisfying *all* the specs of the creative task at hand. They read the fine print and make sure it is satisfied. They catch all your mistakes. Don't be embarrassed; be grateful.

Which role should you play on a creative team?

The creative team role you enjoy most may not be the one you do best. In fact, your favorite role may be the one you wish you did better, or it may be the one you admire others for doing well. Which role do you think you actually perform the best? Your best role isn't necessarily the one *you* do better than everyone else but rather the one you do better than any of the other roles. What makes you good at this role? What skills and personality traits help you to perform this role well? Notice the thoughts, actions, and communications that make you effective in this particular role. Intentionally absorb these behaviors into your default practice and develop the ability to access them during high stress or low confidence situations. Many of us also have a strong second skill. This comes in handy when you find yourself in a group where someone else can capably fill your best role, but there is no one available to fill your second role. This presents a chance for you to step up and shine, and to practice and perfect your second skill.

What happens if your creative collective doesn't have anyone to fill a particular role?

The vultures in Disney's version of *The Jungle Book* famously fall into a loop of asking each other, *What you wanna do?* This question loop keeps them from settling on a course of action. This can happen in your group when you don't have a generator. Everyone ends up asking everyone else what the group should do, but no one seems to have any ideas. Or maybe your group has plenty of generators but no developers. You find yourselves with a plethora of good ideas and no notion of how to advance any of them toward a viable design. Or maybe, everything has gone fabulously, except now, you need someone to check over and refine what's been created, and no one in your group has the patience or the skill to uncover the little mistakes or omissions that have the potential to completely tank your creation. You have to step up, as a collective. You need to join together to become the polisher or the developer or the generator, or whatever role is missing. It may be true that none of you can excel at the missing role on your own but you can accomplish the tasks of the role *together*. If each of you contributes what you are able – one person checks grammar, another size requirements, another accessibility, and so on – you can effectively become a joint version of the missing role. You may not excel, but together, you will be sufficient. Don't just cross your fingers and hope it works though; proof and reproof. And remember to breathe. This will help you not to rush. You're not trying to *get done*; you are attempting *to do*. The first approach – *trying to get done* – zaps you into the future before you're prepared to be there. The second – *attempting to do* – keeps you in the present until you have finished all the necessary tasks.

Notice and benefit from your group's collective rhythm.

Some groups are filled with outwardly calm individuals who all internally contemplate their ideas during each stage of the group's creative process, and then quietly share them one at a time with the entire group. Other groups' members loudly offer their ideas in such a rush they almost speak over each other. Other groups cycle back and forth from quiet to loud moments during their process. Some groups do every step together. Others work individually on different aspects of their task and then work together to develop what each member brings to the table. There is no one ideal group rhythm or process. There *is* a rhythm that is ideal for each group. The ideal rhythm for your group will depend a great deal on who comprises your group: introverts or extroverts; visual thinkers or text-based thinkers; fast or slow processors; those who process by writing or by talking; confident or cautious individuals; or any mixture in any ratio of any of the above. But regardless of the individual characteristics of the members of your group, your group will have a unique rhythm because of the *combination* of individuals in your group. All that matters is that your group's rhythm works for all its members. If you each become intentionally aware of your group's rhythm and honor it, it can make everything flow much more freely and effectively.

SUGGESTIONS
for fostering effective creative teamwork

Suggestion 1:
Behaviors that can help to increase trust and synergy

Discuss basic rules of engagement including: chosen methods of communication; acceptable and unacceptable behaviors; criteria and circumstances for acceptance or dismissal of ideas; desired speed of ideation advancement; level of agreement needed for making major decisions; and expectations concerning acknowledgment and ownership.

- Each team member should clearly communicate which roles they feel most confident filling.
- The team should plan how to cover the absence of any specific team role skills.
- Each team member should clearly communicate the conditions that support and deter their individual creative process, and be vigilant about anything they may unconsciously permit to negatively affect them when working as part of a creative team.
- The team should problem solve to design a creative environment that will work reasonably well for everyone and cause no one undue hardship.
- The team should notice the rhythm and flow of their collective creative process as they begin to work together and devise ways to acknowledge and support the group's process.
- Each team member should strive to use their individual differences to support the group's collective process.

- Each team member should focus on helping the group achieve its creative goals, rather than on advancing their own recognition or demonstrating their superiority.

Suggestion 2:
Behaviors to avoid

Cutting off an idea

This takes place when one member offers an idea and another member begins to loudly, and perhaps excitedly, attempt to force-feed a different idea to the group without first letting everyone hear what the other person is saying.

Try this instead – Patiently allow your teammate adequate time to describe their idea in enough detail to make it possible for the rest of the group to discover if it is viable or worth further exploration.

Overwriting an idea

This takes place when one group member offers an idea and another member eagerly repeats the idea, as if they are endorsing it in its original form; however, they change it substantially or completely as they redeliver it to the group.

Try this instead – Respectfully offer your altered or new idea as a potential alternative to the original version. You can be excited and energetic but do not kill or belittle the other person's idea in order to get yours across. If you are morphing the original idea into something slightly different, acknowledge the aspect of the original idea you are connecting to and developing further. If you are leaping to a totally new idea, identify the aspect of the original idea that inspired you to consider going in a completely different direction.

Overruling an idea

This takes place when one member's idea is immediately dismissed as unacceptable. Overruling is usually done in an abrupt and callous manner that belittles the person offering the idea.

> Try this instead – Help the group parse out why particular aspects of an idea don't work. Stay open to the possibility you may be missing something beneficial about an idea you think is a dud. Try to leap from a positive aspect within the original idea to construct an alternative to those characteristics you consider problematic.

Stopping leapers before they land

This takes place when someone interrupts another person using one idea as a mini-trampoline to spring toward a totally new idea. This disrupts the leaper's creative flow midair, causing them to lose their way and to be unable to land anywhere useful.

> Try this instead – Be patient and wait for the reveal. Acknowledge and explore the new ideas generated by this process.

Leaving negative modeling unchecked

This takes place when the group ignores a negative behavior executed by one of its members. Failing to call out the behavior is often perceived as silent approval. This appears to grant permission to others in the group to engage in similar behaviors.

Try this instead – Choose to model positive behaviors, and to acknowledge them when you notice their presence in the group. Constructively point out negative practices and suggest alternatives, or remind everyone of the group's already agreed upon rules of engagement.

Attempting to force or berate others into staying on track

This takes place when one or more group members insist a teammate is clueless about what needs to happen next. It usually involves talking down to the teammate in a know-it-all manner. Choosing to immediately chastise a teammate for going in the *wrong* direction could prevent the unexpected discovery of outstanding ideas and solutions.

Try this instead – If you are concerned someone is going off on an unfruitful tangent, direct them back by connecting to any aspects of what they are saying that *do* fit what is needed. Then you can point out, if still necessary, why you think other aspects of what they have presented are not a good fit.

Devolving into mutual bemoaning

This takes place when the group uses their limited time and energy to complain about what isn't working, or the unreasonableness or unfairness of their task. This behavior may adversely interrupt the creative flow, result in a decrease in individual confidence, and hamper a willingness to be vulnerable. All of these things can thwart inventive thinking.

Try this instead – Pause your process to acknowledge any difficulties and to affirm your shared confidence in each other's abilities. Adding a healthy dose of humor can be highly beneficial.

Expecting everyone to think and process the same way

This takes place when one member ignores, devalues, rejects, or is irritated by any aspect of another teammate's creative process simply because it is different than their own. One member may be irritated by how quickly or slowly another member speaks when they present their ideas. They may also be annoyed by how verbose the presenter is, or by the level of vocabulary used. A team member who processes internally might lose patience with one who needs to develop their thoughts aloud.

> Try this instead – Reject the temptation to immediately assume anyone who doesn't think or process the way you do is either less intelligent or less capable. Also guard against overcompensating for one team member's needs to the point of compromising the group's collective creative process.

Suggestion 3:
Counterintuitive considerations

Disagreement can be good

You and your team members should always be aiming for the same goal, but you don't always need to agree. Disagreement is often a sign of exploring multiple ways to arrive at the same good solution, or of generating multiple good solutions to satisfy the same goal.

Being annoyed can help you go beyond your comfort zone

Choosing to do a little self-discovery when you notice you are feeling irritated can actually point you toward beneficial ideas you might otherwise have missed. Perhaps you find yourself being annoyed by an idea one of your teammates presents to the group. If you figure out what it is about the idea that rubs you the wrong way – perhaps you realize their idea is likely to confuse the intended audience – you could choose to use this discovery to tweak their idea, instead of feeding your own irritation. This could result in their idea maintaining all of its good points *and* becoming more easily understandable to target users. Or upon further reflection, you may realize one of your teammates hopes to be seen as clever and is rushing to suggest an idea without adequately considering its ramifications. Instead of allowing your annoyance to cause you to kneejerk reject a potentially good idea, you could choose to offer a supportive invitation for everyone to further develop the original idea together.

Competition isn't always a good (or a bad) thing

Healthy competition among group members can spur everyone toward doing their best. Good-natured humor, when seen by all as such, can encourage teammates to continue to improve their performance. Unhealthy competition can damage the group's working relationship and their ability to produce excellence. Intention is often a good litmus test for determining whether a particular instance of competition is good or bad. Is the purpose of the competition to help the group get closer to fulfilling their mission? Or, is one group member attempting to prove their worthiness or to outshine others? Indulging behaviors that derail the group's advancement toward accomplishing their current task with distinction is rarely a good thing.

Being nice doesn't always mean holding back

Being worried about offending someone shouldn't keep you from expressing your hesitations about a proposed idea. Being overly concerned about being judged shouldn't keep you from sharing your own ideas. While it is important to be willing to share, *how* and *why* you communicate are equally as important. Fear of being rude shouldn't stop you from making useful contributions to the group. Just be sure your goal *is* to be useful. You don't have to be belligerent to be insistent. Keep in mind that it is also possible to use nice (non-rude) words to attempt to make someone else look bad. Check your language and your intentions. Then speak up.

Notes:

Stand up and out.

Years ago, my dad told me many people believe sex is the most important thing in a marriage. "It's just not true," he said. Then he smiled and added, "But sex *is* a very big part of a good marriage." The excellent idea you ultimately choose to use to achieve the goals of your creative pursuit is a lot like good sex in a marriage – it alone is not enough to guarantee success. You also need to be able to clearly communicate your idea to others: to any decision-makers who have the power to greenlight your idea; to those who control the funding for your idea's journey into creation; and to the end users or viewers who will ultimately choose whether or not to pay attention to or purchase the final version of your envisioned creation. And before all of this, you have to convince your teammates or partners to invest their creative abilities in the hard work required to develop your idea.

If others have to work to understand your idea, they may tire of the effort and give up. If you can't communicate your idea simply and clearly, there's a good possibility no one will take it seriously. Famous creatives already well-known in their fields are often the only ones who automatically receive the courtesy of a patient listen whenever their ideas are initially unclear to others. New creatives? Not so much. A creative who recently has promoted a not-quite-so-well received idea? Their window of opportunity will only be cracked slightly open. They'll need to quickly slip through something that shines brightly and obviously in a way that will get everyone's attention. The sad reality is that someone else with an almost-but-not-quite-as-good idea as yours, who happens to be a much better communicator than you, will be more likely to have their idea accepted than you will. Why? Because it's human nature to not want to expend a large amount of effort trying to understand something. Why? Because not understanding has a tendency to make people feel stupid. Not a good environment for pitching an idea. A few seconds of confusion is fine, but that confusion needs to quickly turn into an *oh-I-get-it* epiphany that leads to a *that's-brilliant* reaction. Otherwise, your pitch is likely to end up morphing into a sinking-ship defense. Scrambling to defend an idea someone has already labeled as *bad* or *sketchy* should not be confused with building comprehension in a point-by-point manner to demonstrate just how fabulous your idea is.

Attitude is important

If you are in defense mode, your passion may be misinterpreted as fear. If decision-makers even smell fear, they may assume it's because you yourself don't fully believe in your idea. This is not a good thing.

Great idea + bad delivery = zero success.

Figure out exactly what you're going to say. Make sure you start with a passionate attitude. It's important for your passion to communicate confidence rather than desperation. Figure out *why* you are excited about your idea. Begin there. Give your audience an enticing glimpse of the overall concept. Then build deeper understanding quickly and simply, major element by major element. Reveal your idea's structure without all the complicated minutiae; there will be time for those details later.

Real life example:

Imagine a friend of yours is attempting to convince you to go on a blind date with one of their other friends. It's someone you've never met. Your friend insists this person is *perfect* for you. You might begin to question just how *right* this person actually is for you if you sense that your friend:

- is more interested in doing a favor for this friend of theirs than finding a good match for you.
- is desperate to find a date for this friend of theirs because they can't seem to find anyone who wants to date them.
- wants to help this friend of theirs get over a negative relationship.

In much the same way as choosing whether or not to say *yes* to a potential blind date *should be* based primarily on the personal qualities of the blind date candidate being considered rather than on how going out with them would satisfy an ulterior motive of the fixer-upper, a presentation of your idea should focus primarily on your idea's merits rather than on satisfying a hidden agenda you are harboring. If your pitch even hints at how clever or talented you are, you may end up souring the decision-maker's impression of your idea. Their irritation with what they see as bragging or conceit may also cause them to miss the genuine appeal of your idea. This is obviously something you want to avoid. Even if you know more about what the decision-maker needs than they do, do not make the mistake of *telling* them that you do. Instead, *show* them why your idea is best for them. Let your presentation demonstrate how amazing your idea is and *why* it's the perfect choice. Lead your audience to choose your idea; do not make the choice for them. Be passionate and convincing without stepping over the line into the role of decision-maker.

Even if you've recently gone through a creative dry spell or if the rest of your team isn't 100% behind an idea you're championing, do not communicate how desperate you are to have your idea accepted. The slightest whiff of desperation may negatively affect decision-makers. Sometimes they will get a gut sense that something is *not quite right* even though they haven't consciously recognized your desperation.

Also be sure to communicate any challenges you think your idea may possibly encounter. Failure to disclose a potential complication, no matter how slight it may be, invites decision-makers to perceive you as either clueless or sneaky. Neither of these judgments casts you or your idea in a favorable light. Present any possible obstacles as surmountable steps on the journey toward achieving the desired outcome of your idea's implementation. An idea presented with no potential challenges or cautions will often be perceived as too good to be true. Communicate your idea as positively as possible while simultaneously painting a realistic depiction of your idea's proposed implementation processes.

Make it simple and make it sticky.

Remember to start by first showing your audience the bones of your idea. These are your idea's major concepts. Choose language that makes each of these concepts stick in your listeners' minds. Then begin to flesh out each one just enough to give your audience an initial understanding of your idea. Next, choose a metaphor that further explains this introductory description. Choose something outside of the topical area of your idea, something everyone in the room is familiar with, perhaps even something from everyday life. Make sure everyone in your audiences gets the metaphor and grasps its underlying meaning. Then continue to flesh out your idea by presenting a little more information about the concepts and factors you have highlighted in the metaphor. Be sure to explain how your idea's components fit together. Watch your audience. Attempt to ascertain whether or not they understand each component and its function, and how the various components come together to create your idea's intended result. Check in with them if you aren't sure your description makes sense to them.

Connect to everyone but continue to anchor back to the primary decision-maker.

Often your idea is pitched to a group that includes one or a few individuals who have more power over the final decision than others in the group do. Make sure you speak to the entire room by looking around to include everyone as you speak; however, be sure you make eye contact with the major decision-makers in the room when you make any especially important points. Anchor each vital aspect of your presentation in this manner. If you *only* look at the most powerful people in the room and ignore everyone else, you risk coming across as either nervous or arrogant. Obviously, neither of these would be a desirable impression to make.

No one likes a desperate or a cocky presenter.

If you appear worried or nervous, your idea stands a higher chance of being prejudged as mediocre or worthless. If *you* don't seem to believe in the merits of your own idea, why should others? If you seem overly confident in an *I-am-the-best-thing-since-sliced-bread* manner, the decision-makers may be quick to lose patience with you. If you want to convey confidence you have to connect to your audience. If you distance yourself by setting yourself apart in a self-centered, superior manner, your confidence may *read* as cockiness. If you connect to your listeners, if you share your skills and your experiences with them in a self-assured manner, you are more likely to come across as confident.

Speaking too quickly is another way of distancing yourself from your audience. When listeners are bombarded with a rush of words, there is no time or space for them to react. While you may not be expecting anyone to respond with comments during your initial presentation, the hope is that listeners will have the opportunity to connect with certain aspects of what you are saying, and then capture these tidbits in their memories or by jotting them down. Be sure to pace your presentation with a tempo that allows your audience to be part of the conversation, even if it is just as actively engaged *listeners*. Fast-paced rhetoric usually feels exclusionary at best, and inferiority cloaking at worst.

If you are presenting your idea as part of a team, be sure no one speaks over anyone else. Plan who will say what and how you will each *connect* your portions together. Discuss ahead of time what you will do if someone forgets an important point. How will you fill in for each other? While it is important to telegraph your mutual excitement for your idea, it is equally important to convey your confidence in and appreciation of each other. If your team seems disjointed your idea may be perceived to be as well.

Be prepared to relate your journey.

Showing how you arrived at your idea can help your audience to understand it more fully. Include a concise version of the highlights of the creative journey that led to your idea. Make it short; don't ask your audience to slog through a blow-by-blow retelling of every step of your creative process. Tell them about the initial spark and some of the domino points along the way. Perhaps include one of the undesirable side paths you managed to avoid. Save the details for any questions that arise at the end of your presentation.

What if what you have to communicate is you?

Sometimes you find yourself in a situation where you have to pitch yourself. Perhaps you are up for a new position. Maybe a decision-maker wants to interview you before allowing you to be part of a new project. Maybe you're trying to convince your co-members in a non-profit organization they really can trust you to create this year's fundraiser. How can you communicate your skills without coming across as either too full of yourself or too good to be believed? Start with something you do well.

Real life example:

Let's imagine you're someone who can maintain your professional composure in just about any situation. You could give examples of scenarios when you've managed to do this. You could be specific about what you did with your facial expressions, your body language, your words, and your tone. Then you could explain how you are aware that being so good at staying composed can backfire. This is how you would demonstrate a little humility and convey your awareness of the flipside of your good traits. You would most likely mention you understand how important it is to communicate passion while still coming across as professional. You would let your audience know you always pay attention to both of these things. Perhaps you would tell them about a time when things almost started to tank because a decision-maker thought you didn't care enough about a project. Then you would tell them what you did to convey your passion while remaining professional in the manner required in that particular situation.

This is how you would show your audience your awareness of the potential pitfalls of your best skills. Communicate your willingness to be vigilant about where things could go astray and your confidence to handle whatever may arise. This will go a long way to convince others they can trust you to do a good job for them. An interviewer or decision-maker will most likely be impressed by your ability to be ready to meet any challenges that may arise as unintended consequences of your best qualities.

Finally, figure out what your superpower is. Seriously. What are you better at than most people? It can be anything. It may be the ability to learn from your mistakes; to course correct without breaking your stride; or perhaps to process multiple pieces of information quickly. Or maybe you excel at making people feel at ease. What do you think other people would say is your superpower? Maybe they see a small part of your bigger picture. For example, they may comment on what a good vocabulary you have, but that may just be a symptom of your ability to clearly communicate an important point in a way that everyone in the room can follow regardless of their base of knowledge. Or maybe you see your ability to calm people down as your superpower, but actually this is a symptom of your ability to help people get past their emotional responses to a place where they can start thinking. Try to view your own superpower in a conceptual way, not just in an evidentiary way. Applying this type of conceptual thinking to how you perceive the positive traits in those around you will help you to reflect on your own abilities in the same manner.

Present your own strengths in a conceptual manner by labeling the overarching skill you possess and then follow up with the specific sub-skills you use to make it all happen. Be sure to include what the effect of these skills looks like. If someone's superpower is making everyone feel comfortable and included in a process, this may break down into skills such as: using body language and speaking tempo to connect and listen in a manner that makes more people feel attended to and heard; using accepting language to re-label and affirm the contributions of others; and using comments and questions to continuously help everyone to refocus the conversation back toward the creative purpose of the meeting rather than to devolve toward assigning blame or judgment in any way. The outcome of this particular superpower and its sub-skills may be twofold: 1) the increased focus and reconnection back to the task at hand allows for increased mental leaps that carry new ideas and resources forward to the process; and 2) the group is likely to be more cohesively on board with what they have created together because everyone will probably feel as if they were part of the process.

Here's a simplified version of the superpower communication formula: present a conceptual framing of your superpower, preferably in one sentence; follow this with a description of the sub-skills you employ to execute your superpower; and finally describe the positive outcomes likely to occur when you wield your superpower. A real life example is always helpful. Be sure not to name any names that should remain private.

If this is a tell-us-about-yourself interview situation you may get to start with your *superpower* and use the sub-skill descriptions to convey your best traits. If it's a more structured environment, you may get an opportunity in the is-there-anything-else-you'd-like-to-add portion of the interview to refer back to the skills you have described as answers to various questions and weave them together to demonstrate and label your superpower.

Finally, you might actually label your best overarching conceptual ability as your *superpower* in the interview, or you may read your audience and know *superpower* is not a word to use with these people. There are lots of other things to call your superpower. Here are a few: *the thing I do best; the way I think I best bring value to most situations; what I have discovered to often be my most important contribution;* or *the way my skills often complement each other (or work in tandem) in a positive manner.* There are many more. Find the words that are *your* words to describe your superpower.

EXERCISES
to help you stand up and out

Exercise 1:
The plot thickens

You'll need another person to help you with this one. Each of you
– separately at first – should choose a well-known movie that is
familiar to you. Don't tell each other what movies you've selected.
On your own, create a conceptual description of the movie you've
chosen. Write this description on a piece of paper. Make sure the
other person doesn't see it. Do not use any specific information in
your description that makes it easy to identify the movie. If one
of you were to write a description of the *Wizard of Oz* you would
not: 1) name Dorothy or any of the other characters; 2) mention
the Land of Oz or Kansas by name; or 3) reveal that a tornado had
taken place. Instead, Dorothy could be called a *young person*. The
Cowardly Lion, the Scarecrow, and the Tin Man could be referred
to as *numerous* (not three) *helpful strangers*. The Wizard could be
represented as *an important person in the community who is smart
but shifty*. The witch could be described as *a powerful person of great
evil*. Glinda could become *a benevolent and powerful person*. The
Munchkins could become *friendly townsfolk*. And of course you
would not say anything at all about the ruby slippers. The monkeys could become *the powerful person's minions*. The young person
(Dorothy) travels *somewhere far away*. You get the idea. Now here's
the tricky part. After you write this conceptually based version of
your chosen movie's plot, being careful to leave out any identifiers,
choose two words to give to the other person as clues. You can roll
dice or do *Rock, Paper, Scissors* to see who goes first. The other player

guesses which movie you've chosen based on these first two words. After their guess, they take a turn telling you their first two words and you try to guess their movie. Each of you should write down the clues you receive, on your own piece of paper. Write the first two words on the first line. Write each new pair of words on the following line. As the turns continue, try to *construct* a sense of the movie being described by rearranging the words and crafting them into phrases or sentences.

Your objective is to identify the other player's movie; however, your primary goal is to help the other person identify the movie you've chosen as quickly as possible. You want them to succeed. When you are done, evaluate how well you identified and communicated the conceptual essence of your movie to the other player. Did the clue words you chose make it easy for the other person to construct a foundational understanding of what your movie was about, or did they end up causing confusion? Is there anything important you forgot to mention? What could you have done differently? What was particularly effective? What didn't work with this player but might have worked with another? How successful were the other player's clue word choices in helping you to identify their movie? Did the way they presented their clue word choices make you think of something you might do differently the next time you play this game?

Exercise 2:
Sticky metaphors

List any metaphors you remember from your own childhood or from teaching children a skill. For example, some children learn to tie their shoes using the *bunny ears* method. They are instructed to make two loops, one on each side, which resemble bunny ears, and then to tie the two together. Most children are familiar with bunny ears. This is why naming the loops this way helps students to learn and to remember. What other childhood metaphors can you remember? Sometimes these metaphors are conveyed in a song or a rhyme. Make a list. Doing this activity with another person can be helpful because you will have some memories and experiences in common but others that will be unique to just one of you. Having to explain a particular metaphor to the other person will help each of you acquire a better understanding of why the metaphor is successful at helping children to learn the identified task.

Next, brainstorm three simple things you could teach a child to do that were not included in the learning metaphors list you just generated. These could be daily tasks or a physical activity. For each skill, break the task down into its simplest actions. Devise a metaphor for each of the steps. Be sure the elements within the chosen metaphors would be familiar to most children. Also, be sure the metaphors clearly communicate the actions required for each step of the task. If you are doing this with a partner, each of you should come up with your own metaphors for each of the agreed upon steps of a given task. Compare and decide which ones seem best at describing the actions being taught.

Children find it easier to remember what they've been taught when the elements of teaching metaphors already exist as part of one of their preexisting neural networks. This means the children do not have to expend energy to learn a metaphor with new elements. The new information can be *attached* to their previous understanding. This makes it *stick* in a way that not only helps them to learn but also to more easily recall what they have learned. This works for adult learners too.

Exercise 3:
The name game

It can be helpful to come up with a silly saying in your mind to help you to remember a name you don't want to forget. This is much more effective if you associate either the whole name or parts of the name with things you are already familiar with, and the connection between the two makes sense to you. Humor or emotion can make the association more memorable. I met a lovely woman at a bus stop in my town. When she told me her name, I found it difficult to remember. I created an associative saying for her first and her last name to help me remember them. For her last name, *Fatuma,* I imagined myself talking to my mom in the house where I grew up. My mom gained some extra weight during menopause. In my associative story I reach down and pinch a little fat by my waist and say, *Fat too, Ma.* This became *Fatuma.* I further imagined myself saying this to my mom from the doorway of my parents' bedroom in my childhood home, which was right around the corner from the spot in the house I used to create an associative story to help me remember my new friend's first name. (I'm not including her first name here for greater privacy.) This helped to link these associative story memories together and make it easier to remember the two names. The nostalgic childhood memories combined with humor also served to make the associations stickier.

Come up with a few names you want to remember. You could google old movie stars or historical figures. Just be sure to choose names you don't already know. Then find a way to help yourself remember the names. Create associative stories for each name. You can also make up an identity story about someone you meet in order to remember their name. For example, if you meet your friend Mary's husband and his name is Jim and he's slim, you may think of him as *Slim Jim*® to remember his name. Perhaps you would tell yourself, *Mary married a Slim Jim.*

Exercise 4:
Play with attitudes

Start with a simple sentence such as: *I don't want to go.* Then think of how you would say this same sentence under different circumstances. This is often used as an acting exercise. If you are doing the exercise alone, simply come up with various situations in which someone might utter this sentence. Then label the emotion you think would go with the sentence in that scenario and attempt to convey the emotion you identified as you speak the sentence. Say it as if you are *scared* to go. Then say it as if you are *terrified* to go. Try communicating *reluctance* to go based on annoyance and then on being *too busy.*

If you are doing this exercise with a partner, say the sentence and ask your partner to guess the emotion you are attempting to convey. How would you say: *I don't want to go* if you really did want to go but thought the other person would be upset at you if you said you did? What about if you didn't want to go because of *how much you would miss* the other person? What if you were *angry* and felt as if you were being forced to go?

Notice your tone, volume, facial expressions, body language, and where you place emphasis in the sentence. Now, do it again and become aware of your connection to the other person. Purposely use all the elements of communication listed above to connect to the other person as much as you can. Get them to guess which subtext or motivation is behind each of your renditions. Then ask them to imagine what possible scenario might cause you to say the sentence in this way. Take turns doing this with each other's sentences. *It's not my fault* is another good sentence to use.

Exercise 5:
Describe another person's superpower

Think of a person you greatly admire. How would describe their *superpower?* Answer the following questions to construct a description of what makes this particular person (we'll refer to her/him as *Sal* here) amazing:

1) What does Sal do better than other people?
2) What makes people notice Sal?
3) Who would play Sal in a movie?
4) If you could bottle three of Sal's best traits what would the label be on each one?
5) When would it be really helpful to have Sal around?
6) What would a bumper sticker celebrating Sal's excellence say?
7) What superhero name would you give to Sal?

Use the information you've generated to write a concise description of Sal's superpower. Include the overarching benefits of Sal's superpower. Sal's superhero name and bumper sticker can probably help you with this. Also include the characteristics and actions Sal manifests that work together to create Sal's superpower. Your answers to the first four questions above will help you with this. Finally, describe a time when you witnessed Sal's superpower. Your answer to number 5 above may help to jog your memory.

Exercise 6:
Describe your own actual or aspirational (real life) superpower

Answer the same questions from Exercise 5 about your own superpower. If you don't think you have a superpower, answer the question for what you would like your superpower to be. This may help you to hone in on what you already do quite well. In either case, use your answers to create a description of your actual or aspirational superpower.

Exercise 7:
First the BONES then the FLESH

Name three specific things you admire or find despicable about a particular person. Use one pithy sentence for each of the three things. Take each sentence and expand it as much as you possibly can. Describe it in excruciating detail. Include lots of examples. Draw analogies to better explain it. Write and write and write until you feel you've exhausted what you can say about each trait or tendency you are describing. When you are done, write a more concise description. Start with your pithy sentence and then use all the details you've supplied to write three or four additional sentences that encompass the most important aspects of the information all those other words provided.

Exercise 8:
Flip sides

Think of positive personality traits you would want a potential friend, romantic partner, or work colleague to have. Make a list of these. Imagine a scenario where each of these so-called positive traits could have a negative impact. Next think of what you perceive to be your best positive traits. Imagine scenarios where these positive traits could also play out in a negative way.

Notes:

Mind your 3 Ps and the Q

The creative thinking process described in this book encourages readers to use their brains' innate tendencies to help improve their thinking. Creative thinking has traditionally been considered to be something *other* than critical thinking, but in reality creative thinking is simply critical thinking done in a more thorough and excellent manner. Critical thinking done not-so-well is done mindlessly – as in defaulting to externally influenced patterns and categorizations instead of intentionally choosing *how* to use your own mind. Those external influences can push you toward conventional and overly frequented paths of thought. Creative thinking invites us to notice any auto tendencies we may have and to intentionally use the brain's natural processes to go beyond these rote forms of thinking, even when certain formulaic patterns of thinking have been presented to us as *creative*. The creative thinking methods suggested in this book can be summarized in the following four action steps.

Be prolific: notice more to locate the best.

If you want to find something truly amazing, be willing to notice more. Make it your normal practice to consistently attempt to see more. Intentionally trying to see *more* makes you less likely to miss something great, something you might have been inclined to skim over or sail past if you were rushing to grab the first or second shiny and seemingly appropriate thing you noticed. This means creative thinkers must be willing to consciously eye-catalogue more of what they encounter in and beyond their immediate surroundings, and also deep within their own memories and experiences. Commit to habitually pulling back the lens and looking beyond where you would usually look, beyond where you assume you'll find what you need. Remember to do this in both the physical and mental spaces you explore. Continue to notice as much as you can, including the thought-bridges that bring you from one particular place to another. Also notice your mental pause places and where they invite you to leap next. Notice what entices you to leap from one idea to another. Notice what satisfies your creative project's *conceptual* needs. Trust your developing ability to recognize the gems, or useful components, within the avalanche of *all* you are noticing. Over time, your recognition speed will improve, especially if you remember to *find* rather than to *force* your efforts.

Be perceptive: pay attention to your process to produce the best results.

Notice your own process. As you shake up your usual thought patterns and purposely disengage from creative business-as-usual, take note of what works best for you. What helps *you* to initiate ideas, to develop them, and to perfect and refine them? Repeat and take advantage of those things. Also notice what slows you down or causes you to spin out of control. Pay attention to what works for others when you are working with a partner or a creative team. Figure out how to meld and optimize the mix of needs and abilities present. Notice what you say to others and to yourself both aloud and inside your head. Notice your rhythms and sticking points. Notice *why* you make the choices you make. Notice when you need to let your subconscious take over for a while. Notice when you have to set boundaries for yourself or act as your own insistent taskmaster or cheerleader. Notice when you've worked too long and need to take a break. Notice when you're on a positive roll and need to keep going.

Be profound: create something superb to fit all your endeavor's requirements.

Sometimes in creative pursuits, just as in love, we choose the first thing (or person) that appeals to us because we are overly eager to believe we have found perfection. Now and then love-at-first-sight turns out to be the best thing ever, but sometimes a stars-in-our-eyes perception may lack clarity, fail to detect the presence of smoke and mirrors, or tend to glorify a single alluring attribute. Resist settling for something merely clever. Keep looking until you find something you can craft into a truly excellent solution for all of your project's needs. Make sure the components of your creation work in harmony with each other or cause positive synergies. Be on the lookout for any unexpected negative consequences or down-the-line domino effects. Remember to consider your audience; make sure they will find your creation graspable and palatable. Shoot for creating something that feels simultaneously familiar and completely unique to those who experience it. The goal is to cause your audience to feel as if they recognize what you have created, even if they don't completely understand why it feels so approachable to them. And also to delight them with something unexpected that challenges them just enough to be interesting but not so much as to be off-putting. This is as true for a successful ad campaign as it is for the perfect gift selection for someone you care deeply about.

Quit at the right moment: know when to stop your process.

Don't stop too soon. Don't say you're done simply because you want to be done. Don't stop too late. Don't keep redesigning or perfecting because you are overly concerned about failure. Trust your instincts. Stay true to your purpose. Recognize when enough is enough, when more is too much, and when now is the worst time ever to stop. It's frustrating when you misjudge a project's doneness, especially when there isn't an opportunity to go back and redo a bad result. It can feel downright soul-sucking, but these failures along with your successes will hone your ability to sense when you are actually *finished.* Eventually you will have a master baker's nose for your creation's readiness level. You won't need to test it; you will just *know.* You will create until your gut tells you to stop.

The Creative Steps:

Step 1: notice

Step 2: explore

Step 3: connect

Step 4: choose

The *See* Key Principles:

Choose to see more.

Notice conceptual connections.

Become aware of your own process.

The *Do* Key Principles:

Be willing to appear ridiculous.

Don't stay on track.

Know when to stop.

Things to try:

Special thanks to:

Ellen Zeman for being a writing mechanics ninja.
(I didn't always follow her advice.)

Kevin Deutermann for all-around excellence boosting.

About Martin Cooper

Martin Cooper is a pioneer in the wireless industry. He invented the portable mobile phone in 1972. He is an advisor to the US Federal Communications Commission (FCC) and two other entities. He has been widely published on the subject of wireless technology and its applications.

About the author

Cinse Bonino is a former professor of Creativity & Conceptual Development with a background in education and the psychology and mechanics of human learning. Cinse does one-on-one awareness sessions (in person and online) to help individuals better define and create the way they want to be in the world. She also presents and leads workshops on: creativity, problem solving, communication, teaching and learning, and personal awareness. Cinse is the author of *The Ride of Your Life: choosing what drives you*, and *Relationship Residue*. She is also the creator of *WISE ASKS* cards – the non-tarot, tarot deck. Cinse lives in Burlington, Vermont, with her cat Melina, and enjoys the time she gets to spend with her son who currently serves in the U. S. Army.

Check out Cinse's offerings at: seechoosedo.com

For more information about *WISE ASKS* go to: wiseasks.com

CPSIA information can be obtained
at www.ICGtesting.com
Printed in the USA
FSHW021903080919
61800FS